JUAN GONZALO CALLEJAS RAMÍREZ

AGAINST WITCHCRAFT

A manual to prevent, diagnose, and counteract the effects of Witchcraft.

ISBN: 978-1-963017-00-7(ebook)

ISBN: 978-1-963017-01-4(Paperback)

ISBN: 978-1-963017-02-1(Hardcover)

Printed in the United Stated of America

I dedicate these pages, logically, to my Lord Jesus Christ and His most holy Mother, who gives me the strength to confront so much evil in this merciless world. After them, I dedicate this to Julieth, a young mother who died due to witchcraft, and on her deathbed, she sent me a message: "Father Juan, I die peacefully, offering my life for my family and for you, as you were the only priest who believed me and committed to fighting against the evil that was done to me. Although God did not allow me to be set free, I die forgiving those who harmed me, and I want you to know that wherever I am, I will plead to God for you and your ministry, that God may protect you and continue to give you strength to help so many others who suffer and die due to

Witchcraft."

Table of Contents

Introduction

In this era of scientific and technological advancements, many people believe that witchcraft is a thing of the past, limited to small pockets of marginalized individuals with low education and resources. In other words, they perceive witchcraft as something confined to the realm of imagination and superstition. They are far from considering it a historical, real, and ongoing phenomenon in our society. However, studies have shown that witchcraft or sorcery exists across all social strata, including among university students and politicians, as depicted in the book "La bruja" by Germán Castro Caycedo.

This book you have in your hands aims to accomplish several objectives. First, it seeks to convince readers that witchcraft is a real phenomenon. Second, it aims to caution those who believe they are immune to it simply because they don't believe in it. In reality, the lack of faith is one of the factors that facilitates the unchecked influence of witchcraft, even among self-proclaimed atheists or agnostics. Third, it provides guidelines for readers to self-diagnose and determine if they have fallen victim to any curses or malevolent acts. And fourth, it offers some elements to counteract the effects of witchcraft.

Furthermore, although my intention is to write for any reader seeking information on this topic, as a Catholic priest, I cannot ignore the skepticism and rationalism with which ecclesiastical authorities view this issue. They have developed such fear of the media that they want to avoid any possibility of being confronted with the excesses of the Inquisition. Therefore, what we will propose in this book is a way to address the issue of witchcraft without going to the extremes of denying its existence or reviving the inquisitorial witch-hunts.

I want to draw the reader's attention to how the mass media increasingly discusses the topic of witchcraft and sorcery. For example, the favorite video games of young people are filled with esoteric languages, symbols, and characters that instruct teenagers in the use of powers and spells. Similarly, the film industry works tirelessly to promote the practice of witchcraft by producing hundreds of movies that showcase the "wonders" of such arts. Likewise, adults are subliminally influenced and indoctrinated through the satanic symbolism they encounter in horror movies.

My experience leads me to assert that witchcraft is much more than a simple figment of the imagination and that in the background of so many novels and movies there is a reality and a danger that should be faced before it is too late.

I also want to use this platform to warn people who are already affected by these kinds of afflictions. I especially recommend that they avoid falling into the temptation of using witchcraft as a method to counteract or undo the harm they are experiencing. The forces of evil will never fight against themselves; that would imply being divided among them, and a divided kingdom cannot prevail. Moreover, all the "countermeasures" created by witches themselves contain another malevolent spell that will affect the person differently in the future, forcing them to return to the source of the evil, creating a kind of dependence or addiction, even to the extent of jeopardizing their entire livelihood.

It is also the intention of this writing to convince individuals that it is not necessary to possess extraordinary powers or extensive knowledge of magical subjects to counteract witchcraft. In fact, magical elements, potions, herbs, or concoctions are not even required to dissolve spells and hexes, instead an act of faith in the power of the one true God is enough, under whom Satan along with all his forces have always been subjugated.

In very few cases, it may be necessary to seek the assistance of an exorcist priest to dissolve most spells. In the majority of cases, prayers and procedures that we will propose in each chapter will suffice. It is necessary to call upon a priest when a high-level witch with Satanic consecration has been Involved in the creation of a malevolent spell. This refers to individuals who hold priestly and episcopal ranks within a diabolical sect. I hope that by placing this book in your hands, I am providing you with an effective tool to protect yourself from what many people prefer to ignore. This is not a matter of superstition but rather a collection of prayers to shield oneself from these forces, whose power I witness daily and have personally been a victim of.

Chapter I
Why I Chose This Path

The reader may wonder why a Catholic priest is discussing a topic that most priests prefer to evade or deny. The reason is that in my youth, I was a victim of the deceptions of the Evil One, and I can even say that I served him.

In this chapter, I want to share with my readers a brief account of my life so that they may understand why I chose to dedicate myself to fighting against the forces of evil. God granted me the grace to see His light amidst the darkness in which I myself was immersed. Since then, I have felt the need to share that light with all those who I know are walking in the midst of the darkness of ignorance.

SWITCHING SIDES BY GOD'S MERCY

Most people believe that every priest is born as one, but that wasn't the case for me. Although I come from a practicing Catholic family, my faith took a turn when I was fourteen years old. I started listening to heavy metal music, and gradually, my attitude towards religion shifted from devout to unbelieving, from unbelieving to atheist, and from atheist to anti-theist. I gradually developed a taste for all things dark and macabre: black clothing, chains, images of demons, zombies, inverted crosses, and animal skins from sacrificial rituals. I also delved into divination, the I Ching, and witchcraft. I bought books on white, green, red, and black magic.

I was studying in a Catholic school, and sadly, it was there that I took the wrong path. My classmates invited me to get involved in the business of selling pornography. We traded in knives and even sold firecrackers for some of the revolts that broke out in the school. Among the materials that came into the school, we received literature on sadism and masochism, Chinese witchcraft, divination, and magic. To feel more confident and tough, I acquired these books and started absorbing their contents to intimidate my friends, not only with the knives I carried but also with the occult subjects I discussed.

It was the difficult nineties in Medellín. Thanks to my inclinations, I found new friends, fellow rockers, but they turned out to be much more than that. The world, the devil, and the flesh held onto me with their serpentine tentacles, submerging me into ever deeper darkness.

My parents' prayers never ceased, and even though they knew it was impossible to talk to me about God without eliciting rebellious and, in some cases, blasphemous responses, they never stopped entrusting me to the Holy Mass and the daily Rosary. Since God never ignores any prayer, He had to make use of a very particular character to make me reconsider the need for reform in my life. This divine messenger is called death.

Certainly, I knew my friends weren't "nuns," as some of them carried weapons and were involved in drug dealing or money laundering, but I had never suspected that they were involved in taking the lives of other human beings. One day, the gang leader, whom we called "Banana" because of his blond and freckled appearance, invited me to accompany him for a business transaction. We arrived at a bar located in Nutibara, near the Antioquia neighborhood, where delinquency thrived in those days. "Banana" started talking to a man with a very sinister face about the value of a "doll," which the thug priced at 600,000 pesos. Since I didn't understand what doll they were talking about, as it seemed too expensive to me, I asked "Banana" about it after we left. He explained it to me like this: "The 'tie' (some executive) wants to

5

'off' (kill) some guy, and I take care of finding him a 'gunman' (hitman) who will do the job. That guy charges me 600,000 'bucks' (pesos), and I charge the 'tie' a 'melon' (million)." At that moment, I realized that my friends were dealing with human lives, but I knew too much to walk away without consequences, so I kept silent and never asked anything about the matter again.

Shortly after, death visited the gang. One of our friends was riding a motorcycle and didn't respect a stop sign. On the other side of the intersection, there was a camper, an off- road vehicle, that collided with him with such force that it severed his leg instantly and threw him ten meters away. Our companion was terribly disfigured, and his family had decided to seal the coffin for the wake. In the midst of our senseless rebellion, we decided to open the lid. As I opened the coffin, I was faced with the distorted face of that young man; his mouth had to be sewn shut because he had died in a scream of pain. His face said to me, "Hell exists, and your friend is in it." I didn't understand it immediately until, amidst drinks, the deceased's best friend told me that he would kidnap policemen and brutally murder them on the outskirts of the city, claiming the $2,000,000 pesos that the infamous drug lord Pablo Escobar paid for each dead police officer using the fallen officer's badge. That news had a profound impact on me because, despite my rebelliousness, I still held onto the respect for life that my parents had instilled in me. It seemed to me that taking someone's life would carry an immense burden of conscience. Such was the impression left on me by that event that, from being the most outgoing member of the gang, I started distancing myself, becoming contemplative and silent.

My transformation was so noticeable that one of my friends asked me what was happening. I told him, "Brother, I can't stop thinking about the burden of conscience one carries when they kill someone." To console me, my friend replied:

"Don't worry, buddy, the only one that hasn't been erased from my memory is the first one, all the others are like killing dogs." And he began to describe to me how his first job went: "Man, I was so scared that I had to get high on marijuana, my buddy took me on his motorcycle to the corner, and from there I walked up to the target. I asked if he was so-and-so, and once he confirmed it, I pulled out the piece (gun) and started unloading on him. I still remember how pieces of brain were falling on the sidewalk, and I was so frightened, man, that even after I ran out of bullets, I kept pulling the trigger empty-handed. I was in such shock that if my buddy on the motorcycle hadn't grabbed me and lifted me up, I would still be standing there, staring at the trail of brains on the street." That confession, which he thought would encourage me and remove my scruples, only fueled the feeling that I shouldn't continue with such companions.

Death was going to keep getting closer because it had been delegated by God to change the course of my life. At a party, "Banana" decided to push me into the center of the dance floor because I didn't want to dance. I fell face-first on the ground like a toad, and everyone started laughing, but I didn't like that, so I reacted by pushing him back. He flew over some tables, knocking over drinks, and falling onto some girls. Then a fight broke out, and all my friends had to react immediately to separate us. But the next day, I received an ultimatum: "Juango, run away because 'Banana' is looking for you to give you a wooden pajama (coffin)." So, I replied, "If he's looking for me, it's better that he finds me because that dog is so treacherous, that he's capable of killing my parents or my girlfriend if he doesn't find me. Besides, you already know who started the fight and who was at fault, so you can decide whose side you're on.

Thanks to the Virgin Mary, who never abandoned me, all my gang friends sided with me and told "Banana" that if anything happened to me, he would be the next corpse, and he had to make

7

peace. Some might find it strange that I mention the Virgin Mary, considering the advanced level of atheism I was in. However, even though I didn't think about the protection of my Heavenly Mother at that moment, later I realized that I always had her in mind. I remembered that on several occasions when my friends started insulting God, blaspheming about Jesus Christ, and saying obscene things about nuns and priests, whenever they were about to talk about the Blessed Virgin, I would stop them, saying that what was with the Virgin was with me, so they shouldn't mess with her. I know it's illogical to detest Jesus Christ and love the Virgin, but that devotion to the Virgin was instilled in me since I was very young, and I could never doubt her existence or the love she felt for me. It's no coincidence that those "what's with her is with me" are the same words my friends uttered when they saved my life, saying, "what's with him is with us."

Although I felt death close on this occasion, there was still a masterstroke from God needed to convince me to change: to come face to face with death. After dropping off one of my five girlfriends at her house, I sped away in my father's SUV, screeching the tires; two blocks away, a bus failed to stop at a stop sign and hit me head-on. The car skidded, with the rear tire exploding against the curb, crashing sideways into a tree. The tree tore through the side of the SUV, shattering all the windows into pieces, and almost completely destroying the vehicle. Miraculously, my body suffered no harm, but my soul had an experience that will never be erased from my memory: I saw images of my entire life flash before my eyes in a matter of seconds, from the moment of my birth to the instant I was being involved in the accident. I realized that everything we do or think is stored in God.

That night, I wanted to pray, but after five years of anti-theism, I had forgotten how to do it. I became desperate because I couldn't even remember the Lord's Prayer or the Hail Mary. My conscience was troubled by the fact that I had to present myself before God with that almost pornographic photo album of my life because even though I respected life, morally and sexually, I didn't respect the temple of the Holy Spirit that is my body. I degraded it through numerous sexual relationships I had, not only with my girlfriends but with every woman who crossed my path. Although I had five official girlfriends, there were many more who succumbed to my seductions.

Amidst my anguish of not knowing how to pray and out of pride, not wanting to turn to my parents so they wouldn't realize how scared I was of how close my death had been, I decided to recite the Creed every day. I asked the chaplain at the University for a Copy, hoping that God would pull me out of the pit I had dug myself into. The response was not long in coming.

My mother invited a charismatic prayer group to my house, and one of the members began sharing all his experiences in deliverance and exorcisms, as the Lord had granted him the gift of sensing the presence of Satan and his fallen angels. I was listening to the conversation from a nearby room, so I came out and asked him to come to my room to see if he could sense the presence of the Devil there. He told me it wasn't necessary because since he had entered the house, he had felt the presence of Satan in my room, but he assured me that we should go in because he was not afraid.

Upon entering and seeing all the walls covered in posters of skulls, demons, skeletons, some drawings of hell that I had made, and real bats nailed to the closet doors, he surprised me with his proposition: "Let's break all of this." What scared me the most was that I wanted to say yes, but it felt as if someone was grabbing me by the throat and not allowing me to speak. However, I managed to find the strength to say, "Do whatever you want."

The man began tearing down all the posters I had pinned to the wall, but what caught my attention was that those nails that I had struggled to remove on previous occasions, causing pieces of the wall to come off, now, under the authority and blessing of this

9

servant of God, were coming out as if they were stuck in butter after he made the sign of the cross over them.

Another gift that surprised me about this consecrated layperson was his ability to perceive, through the closet doors, things contaminated by Satanism. He pointed out the places where I kept my rock music, which I was made to burn; all my shirts with satanic prints, which were also destined for the fire, and even the hidden place where I had my books on witchcraft locked away.

My astonishment reached its peak when, upon requesting the Holy Scriptures for a deliverance prayer, as soon as he touched the sacred book, he said, "You must have done something to this Bible because I feel it weighing heavy." I argued that I didn't remember doing anything to it and that I had never been interested in the word of God due to my antitheistic stance. Suddenly, I recalled that several years ago, I had bought an album by the band Iron Maiden titled "The Number of the Beast," which featured a citation from Revelation 13:18 on the cover: "Here is wisdom. Let him who has understanding calculate the number of the beast, for it is the number of a man: His number is 666." In my youthful enthusiasm, I had underlined those Bible verses with a red pen, believing that they demonstrated Satan's triumph over God. This hatred for everything divine and my Satanic rebellion caused that page of the Bible to become spiritually contaminated. The charismatic layperson could perceive this sacrilege and had to proceed to tear out the page before beginning the readings that would initiate my liberation.

They imposed a crucifix on my back, and I felt a negative presence retreating from me, while a spiritual fire descended upon me, burning within me with an indescribable flame of peace and harmony, filling me with a love for God as I had never felt before. At that moment, I decided to change my life and do everything in my power to not lose the peace I had felt during my liberation. So I asked these laypeople what I should do to maintain that peace, and they told me that I should pray the Rosary daily. I gladly committed myself to this practice, along with my father and mother. They also advised me to attend Holy Mass regularly, as the presence of Christ within us is essential to prevent the return of Satan into our lives. I gladly made this commitment as well. However, when they proposed that I should confess my sins to a priest, I told them that I had no reason to confess to a human being who is just as sinful as I am. But they argued that if I didn't confess, I would lose that peace.

I made several attempts to join the confession line, but each time I was close, I would postpone it for the following Sunday. Until one day, I said to myself, "Why should I, a gang member, fear a mere priest when I had a gun in my mouth and didn't flinch? If the priest scolds me, we'll both be rolling down the stairs, throwing punches." Thankfully, the priest treated me with great kindness, and not only was there no need for violence, but a friendship began to develop as he started advising me on how to improve my life. From that moment on, I started attending groups of young people in the Catholic Charismatic Renewal, where I learned more about the Word of God and had the opportunity to evangelize by sharing my conversion testimony. I also had the chance to meet priests within the Renewal who had the power to heal the sick and liberate the possessed, and I gradually became involved in assisting them in exorcisms and deliverance ministries.

With time, a desire arose within me to become a priest like them, so I could help people oppressed by the forces of evil more effectively. I decided to dedicate a year of my life to God to discern with certainty whether I was called to marriage or priesthood. During that year, I wanted to suspend all worldly contact and fully dedicate myself to evangelization. For this purpose, I postponed my university studies because I was in my fourth semester of Electronics Engineering. This way, if the priesthood wasn't for me, I could resume my studies without losing the money my father had invested. When I announced this decision at the university, my friends and professors opposed it, recommending other paths such as the diaconate or serving God through my profession. Faced with so many opposing opinions, I decided to separate myself from all my worldly friends and focus solely on the friends within the Catholic Renewal.

Many people believe that when one receives a calling to serve God, all paths become smooth and mystical, and all difficulties disappear just because one wants to serve God. But in reality, it's the opposite. That's when the devil, the world, and the flesh attack, tempt and wound with greater animosity. For example, when I proposed to my parish priest that I would leave everything for a year to discern a priestly vocation, he advised me strongly against it, saying that priesthood was very demanding and that it would be better for me to marry the beautiful girlfriend I had and then ask God what He wanted from me. We shouldn't judge my parish priest's advice negatively because he knew about my disorderly life, and although I now had only one girlfriend, until a few months ago, I had been involved with five girls at the same time, and that's why my spiritual director didn't see much future in my priestly chastity. Despite this lack of support from my spiritual director, I decided to move forward with that year of discernment because I have always believed that dedicating a year to God's service cannot have negative effects on a Christian's life, but rather will always be enriching.

So I decided to share the news with my girlfriend about the determination I had made; she didn't take it well, but I had to continue on my path. A few days later, I went to visit her and was surprised to find out that she had attempted suicide. Her mother told me that she had thrown herself down the stairs due to the pain of our breakup. That's when my doubts began about whether it was right to leave her or if I should postpone my year of discernment. I then entered into prayer before the Blessed Sacrament, asking for guidance in this difficult situation. The Lord granted me great peace to continue forward and I asked Him to bear the consequences of my vocational search. I was surprised by the speed of the response because the next day my ex-girlfriend called me to say that the Lord had told her that He wanted me on this path and that she had no right to come between us. I didn't have the courage to ask her how He had told her, but I thanked the Lord internally for making His path so clear.

However, that didn't mean that the temptation of the flesh would just disappear, as a few days later, the old vampires from my past life began to reappear, telling me how much they missed me. In fact, even a friend supposedly called to ask for a favor, and when I asked what it was, she responded that she wanted me to take her virginity. In that manner, there were numerous temptations that were placed in my path, but with the Grace of God, I was able to evade them.

After that year, I consecrated myself to God, dedicating my life to praying for people who were oppressed by Satan as I once was. God opened doors for me to study in Spain and go on missions to various parts of the world, fighting to end the empire of the one who once had me enslaved under his sinister claws. I vowed to my Lord Jesus Christ that I would use my knowledge of the dark arts to wage war against the prince of this world and create an army of brave and self- sacrificing souls dedicated to fighting for the liberation of those enslaved by Satan.

The Battle Begins

Despite all the struggles I faced on my journey to priesthood, I never imagined that after being ordained as a priest, my battles would become even greater and against those I least expected to confront.

Against Ecclesiastical Authorities

One of the worst struggles I have had to face as a charismatic and exorcist priest is the lack of understanding, coldness, and disdainful ignorance from the bishops regarding our apostolic activities.

I remember on one occasion a woman who exhibited signs of demonic possession invited me to have lunch with her husband. After we ate, she asked me to say a little prayer of deliverance because she had been feeling very ill for many years. As I began to invoke the Blood of Christ, the woman collapsed, started writhing, and her voice changed. She told me not to meddle with him because I had committed such and such sins. Then, she began to vomit a transparent froth in such quantity that I had to ask her husband to bring a bucket, which the poor woman filled halfway with her transparent vomit.

Since I didn't have permission from the Diocese to perform an exorcism, I immediately went to the Bishop's office to explain the case and request authorization to perform the exorcism or have the Diocese's exorcist attend to her. In response to my request, I was summoned before a kind of tribunal composed of a priest psychologist, a psychiatrist, and two psychologists. They determined that the woman was neurotic and, therefore, an exorcism should not be performed on her. In that moment, filled with righteous anger, I stood up and addressed the priest psychologist, asking him not to insult me because I also had my own studies. Nowhere does it say that neurosis can cause a person to confess sins known only to their confessor and God, or to produce selective vomiting. After eating and drinking in front of me, that woman filled the bucket halfway, without expelling a single particle of what she had consumed just five minutes earlier. I also assured him that no psychiatric illness could cause a person to speak languages they had never studied. That woman had addressed me in perfect Latin, Greek, furthermore, she spoke to me in Aramaic and two other Slavic languages whose origins I couldn't even determine. Therefore, I demanded, as a duty of the Diocese, that she be given immediate spiritual assistance. Because if I had the slightest doubt that it could be merely a psychological disorder, I would not have approached the Diocese seeking this kind of help; instead, I would have referred her to my psychologist and psychiatrist friends who could have provided more professional assistance.

In fact, I presented a report from a Catholic psychiatrist friend who had conducted the most complex tests developed in German psychiatry to determine without a doubt whether a person had a psychiatric disorder. This psychiatrist made the note that in none of the tests did any evidence emerge of the woman having any psychiatric disorder, and based on the manifestations he had witnessed himself, he recommended that she be subjected to the prayers of exorcism, as these prayers, in his view, would not harm a person, even if they had a mental disorder. At the very least, if the affected person requested it, they would feel heard, attended to, and assisted with this spiritual help, especially considering this woman for whom her extensive sessions had never provided any evidence of a psychiatric disorder.

With this ace up my sleeve, which, of course, this tribunal of psychological inquisition did not expect, I argued that I found it utterly unprofessional to label a person as neurotic after only speaking with her for twenty minutes, especially when a professional psychiatrist, after months of treating her and conducting scientific examinations, had not found any disorder in her.

I told the priest that if the bishop used him as an excuse to avoid the inconvenience of dealing with these cases, he should be aware of the account he would have to give to God for closing the doors of the Church to so many desperate people who were truly

15

affected by a spiritual illness that only the prayers of the Holy Mother Catholic Church could heal. The case was that, upon being defeated by my arguments and evidence, they agreed to refer her to the "exorcist" of the Diocese. When the woman finished her first session, I asked her how it went, and she replied that she was fine, but the "exorcist" wasn't, as he had only laid hands on her and said, "Daughter, don't think about the devil anymore, as those things won't help your psychological health." Then he started a simple prayer that he couldn't finish because the legion inside the woman manifested itself and threw that charlatan over his desk.

When I contacted the so-called "exorcist," the first thing I asked him was whether he had used the exorcism ritual, and he said he had never possessed one and asked if I could send him a copy just in case they sent him another crazy person like the one they had sent him. The second thing I asked him was how long he had been the exorcist of the Diocese, and his response was that there had never been an exorcist in that Diocese, and since he was the parish priest of the cathedral, the bishop had instructed him to handle the neurotic woman at my insistence.

It is sad to see that in the Catholic Church today, we see reflected in the shepherds of the Church the attitudes that Jesus condemned in the parable of the Good Samaritan (Luke 10:30-ss), where Jesus says: "that a man fell into the hands of robbers, who stripped him, beat him, and went away, leaving him half dead. As a priest happened to be going down the same road, and when he saw him, he passed by on the other side. Likewise, a Levite, when he came to the place and saw him, passed by on the other side. But a Samaritan, as he journeyed, came to where he was, and when he saw him, he had compassion. He went to him and bound up his wounds, pouring on oil and wine. Then he set him on his own animal and brought him to an inn and took care of him." Jesus, at the end of this parable, asked who among the three was the neighbor to the man who fell into the hands of robbers. I also ask modern bishops and priests if they consider themselves neighbors to those who have been robbed by those robbers who are witches and beaten with a multitude of spiritual illnesses by the sorcerers, or if they simply, like the priest in the parable, take a detour and excuse themselves by claiming it is a psychiatric illness to avoid the effort of the lengthy prayers of the exorcism ritual. Likewise, I ask modern theologians if they, too, will take their detour like the Levite, excusing themselves for not having the necessary permissions to attend to these poor sheep, or if they will take refuge behind a rationalistic theology that denies the ability of the devil to possess people's bodies.

Returning to our story with a heavy heart, upon witnessing the ineptitude with which spiritual matters were handled in that Diocese, I decided to seek a committed bishop who would share in the suffering of these souls, as I did. Although it required us to travel more than 150 km, I managed to obtain the necessary permissions to perform the exorcism on this poor woman. The sessions were long and exhausting,

For casting out a legion is not a simple matter, but those who place their trust in God will quickly see the assistance that comes from the Lord. Thus, amidst loud screams, death threats against my person, and blasphemies against God, the Virgin Mary, and the Holy Mother Catholic Church, these thousands of fallen angels had to retreat in the face of the strength of the Church, represented by a man as wretched and sinful as myself. From that moment on, I made a promise to my Lord that I would never abandon a soul in need of my ministry, as long as the Lord granted me the strength to confront Satan and his followers, and that I would not be discouraged by the disdainful attitudes of some members of the Catholic Church. For them and for all those who doubt the existence of the devil, who think that everything can be reduced to mental disorders, it must be assured that the reality is undeniable—that what they call psychiatric illnesses are treatable and completely curable through prayers of liberation, while illnesses that are truly the result of mental disorders are never cured, but rather palliative care is provided through psychotropic medications. Another argument to assert that diabolical possession is not a psychological illness is the fact that exorcisms can be performed at a distance, even without the person's knowledge, and yet the afflicted individual exhibits manifes- tations at the exact same time when those prayers are conducted remotely. I cite the case of Saint Gemma Galgani as an example, to whom her spiritual director, the Passionist Father Germano of San Estanislao, was performing exorcisms on her while he was in Rome and she was in Lucca, despite the confessor bishop of the saint, Monsignor Volpi, attributing the diabolical phenomena she experienced to hysteria. For more details, we invite our readers to read the autobiography of this Italian saint who died in Lucca in the year 1903, stigmatized like Father Pio.

Returning to the topic we were discussing, if it were psychological illnesses, the presence of the patient would be necessary at least to create the necessary suggestion that would serve as psychic therapy to achieve the normalization or psychic stability of the person.

I would like to propose the following points for reflection: most people believe that no one can perform an exorcism without being authorized by the bishop of a diocese, but in reality, Jesus says in Luke 9:49-50 and Mark 9:38-40: "Do not stop him" (when John told Jesus that they had tried to stop someone who was not one of the twelve or their disciples from performing exorcisms). From this Gospel text, we see that it is the right of every Christian, especially every pastor who wants to defend his flock from the wolves that seek to seize the sheep. We must understand the restrictions of the Church hierarchy in this way: anyone who wants to exercise ministry in the name of the Catholic Church and using the official rituals of the Church must have the approval of a bishop to avoid excesses and potential harm (Canon 1172). However, at no time can the Church restrict the prayer of liberation performed by priests, faithful Catholics, and Protestant pastors if the prayer being offered is not part of the official ritual and is not done in the name of the Church. But in virtue of the charisms received from Christ and the authorization given by Jesus in Mark 16:17, when He says, "And these signs will accompany those who believe: In my name, they will drive out demons..."

If they were to prohibit it, they would not be acting as representatives of Christ but as antagonists of Christ, who commands the expulsion of demons as one of the clearest signs that the kingdom of God is among us, and that defeating the devil was one of the main reasons that moved the Son of God to incarnate, for according to 1 John 3:8, the Son of God appeared to destroy the works of the devil.

The other point of reflection, for those who believe in the divinity of Jesus Christ but think that Christ was actually dealing with mentally ill individuals when facing the possessed, is as follows: if Satan is merely a psychiatric anomaly, this would imply that Jesus Christ is either not God or not a teacher. Let me explain: if Jesus Christ was performing exorcisms while actually dealing with psychiatric illnesses, then He Himself was mistaken, and as we know, God cannot make mistakes. Moreover, the pinnacle of error would have been reached when He engages in a dialogue with a supposed psychological illness, asking (Matthew 8:28-32), "What is your name?" and the alleged illness responds, "Legion, for we are many." It would be even more absurd for the Gospel to claim that a psychological illness asked Jesus to let it enter into a herd of swine, and it would be reaching the height of the utopian to suggest that Christ authorized a psychological illness to cause a loss of reason in swine that never possessed reason to begin with.

I say He would not be a teacher if, as some convoluted theologians claim, if Christ, knowing it was a psychological illness, acted as if He were dealing with a demon to accommodate the idiosyncrasies of the Jewish people, He would have failed in the basic duty of every teacher, which is to correct the supposed error of that people by teaching them that it was not about demons but simply psychological imbalances. Consequently, He would have ceased to be the Way, the Truth, and the Life. Moreover, the verses in the Gospels that affirm that Christ healed the mentally ill and the possessed confirm that the Jewish people could differentiate between someone with a mental disorder and someone possessed by a demon.

It is unfortunate that the shepherds of the Catholic Church do not consider the terrible pastoral consequences for the people of God entrusted to them. If a person who feels affected by oppression, obsession, or demonic possession turns to their bishop and is immediately labeled as crazy by that pastor, they will obviously seek a solution to their spiritual problem elsewhere. I recall the case of a young man who had been tormented by demonic nightmares, preventing him from sleeping for weeks and causing extreme physical exhaustion. In his desperation, he went to a bishop asking for deliverance so that he could rest. The bishop simply told him, "Your problem is that you're eating too late, and that's why you're having those nightmares. So it's better not to eat before going to bed," and sent him home.

It is understandable that a Catholic who feels mocked in such a manner would seek a solution to their problems from a Protestant pastor or, in the worst case, from a witchdoctor.

I would like the bishops to reflect on the fact that if a person seeks a spiritual solution for their spiritual problems from a Protestant pastor and finds it, their reaction will inevitably be to say, "If this Christian Church believed in me and prayed for me until I found liberation, why should I go to the Catholic Church where bishops and priests think they are doctors or psychiatrists and have lost their vision and mission as spiritual physicians?" What is even more disheartening is when faithful Catholic, in their desperation, feels compelled to resort to magic and witchcraft to alleviate their

20

spiritual suffering. In that case, all they do is further harm their soul because, as the Lord clearly states in the Gospel, Beelzebub cannot cast out Beelzebub.

To give an example, a peasant woman came to me after being subjected to a spell of illness. She had sought medical help, but the doctors couldn't determine the supernatural origin of her ailments, and the priests did not acknowledge it either. In her desperation, she made the grave mistake of turning to one of the mediums of José Gregorio Hernández in search of bodily healing. Unfortunately, not only did her condition worsen, but she also lost a large sum of money they charged her. This case was quite challenging to liberate because her visit to José Gregorio intensified the destructive power of the illness, and I believe that, due to that mistake, her recovery will never be optimal.

Against Envy

Another struggle that every exorcist must face is the battle against their fellow priests within the priesthood. The role of an exorcist not only attracts those affected by the devil but also numerous curious individuals who seek novelty. This, in turn, leads to unfounded envy from their fellow priests.

When I began my ministry of liberation, I was assigned to a micro chapel of 4.5 square meters in a sector of a parish that even the parish priest himself didn't want to visit due to its dangerous nature. The police wouldn't even enter that neighborhood. Months after my arrival, I was the only person in the entire town with a daily attendance of over thirty people, except on Sundays, when up to four hundred people would come, requiring us to celebrate outdoors. Since the other priests in the town only had the attendance of the same four elderly ladies at daily Mass, they began to wage war against me, claiming that I was taking away their parishioners and income. They also accused me of being a charlatan who deceived people with potions, which were actually sacramentals: water, salt, and exorcised oil.

Sacramentals are items with a special blessing that have been used throughout the history of the Church to repel the attacks of the devil, the world, and the flesh. They have a spiritual significance rooted in Sacred Scripture: water symbolizes our baptism, oil symbolizes the anointing of the Holy Spirit, used in Scripture for the appointment of priests, prophets, and kings. As for salt, Jesus Christ said, "You are the salt of the earth" (Matthew 5:13), referring to its ability to prevent the decay of flesh. Once blessed by a priest, it will prevent spiritual corruption caused by Satan.

The use of these elements as protection is far from the superstition with which herbalists and healers use natural elements to cause a spiritual effect.

At first, I was greatly discouraged by such judgments, but over time, I stopped paying attention to them. When one treats the priesthood as if it were running a convenience store that opens half an hour before Mass and closes in the face of poor parishioners who want to pray a little, that is not being a priest, but rather a mere public official. A priest is someone who cares about the spiritual well-being of his flock, even if it entails long hours of prayer and facing spiritual wolves that, in some cases, can cause severe wounds to the person of the shepherd.

Against the Demons

It may seem obvious to say that every exorcist faces the Devil, but I would like to share some of the ways in which the Devil has targeted me over the years of confronting him, so that it is not assumed that we enjoy diplomatic immunity against the enemy's attacks. The most common methods of intimidation are to appear stronger than he actually is and to attack the priest's weakest point.

I remember that in my early days, the demon used to visit me by knocking on my bedroom door at three in the morning when he knew I was alone in the rectory. To not be intimidated, I would get out of bed and open the door, but obviously, there was no one there. So, I would try to go back to sleep, but then there would be knocking on the ceiling of my room, followed by footsteps beside me.

This went on for several days, until fed up with the prank, I would simply shout, "Go to hell and let me sleep."

I have also been repeatedly threatened with death and told that when I return to my hometown, I will find my mother dead, as they always threaten to attack what one loves the most. I calmly respond that the only owner and lord of life is my Lord Jesus Christ. It has become so common that I joke with my mother, saying, "Mom, you know that in the last exorcism, the demons sent you off to the afterlife." And she replies, "Don't worry, son, they can only do what God allows them to, and in case God gives them permission, I've already bought a one-way, non-stop flight ticket to purgatory, thanks to my daily rosary."

Another tactic of the demons is to tempt priests with the issue of the flesh, and I have to admit that they have good allies for that. I have had to dismiss two of my secretaries because they proposed marriage to me, not to mention the times they have flirted with me in the confessional, regardless of my receding hairline and potbelly. The demon doesn't sleep, doesn't rest, doesn't waste time eating, so he can spend hours analyzing the exorcist until he discovers their tiniest weaknesses. Once he discovers them, he will attack day and night until he succeeds, if not prevented by the Virgin and Jesus Christ.

Against Witches

I have often stated that I am more concerned about witches than demons. This is because the fallen angel himself is limited in his actions by the divine will. As we see in the Book of Job, they have to seek permission in each case to cause harm. On the other hand, the sorcerer has human freedom that God respects, and this freedom gives the demons a green light to attack, tempt, and harm. In fact, if there were no witches, the power of demons would be so limited that we would practically have them as harmless pets.

The critical aspect of the current situation is that most Catholics believe that witchcraft is not effective or that it belongs to the realm of fairy tales. However, witchcraft is an art that has developed astonishing spiritual techniques to cause harm, ruin, and even death to its victims.

It is not uncommon to find infiltrators in prayer groups, seminaries, and convents who are members of satanic sects or witch covens. They subtly inject the satanic poison of discord, envy, and pride into these environments. I recall the case of an exorcist priest who, after liberating a witch, associated her with his team without realizing that her liberation was staged, and she ended up seducing him to the point of making him abandon his religious habits. I have also experienced the infiltration of a witch among the members of my ministry. This individual not only tainted my food with their potions, leading me to the point of urinating blood but also turned the members of my liberation team against me. As a result, out of forty servants of the Lord, I was left with only three.

I could entertain you with numerous occasions when witches have infiltrated the events I have conducted, trying to spread their filth among the people who come seeking liberation. However, the Lord has taught me not to give them too much prominence. So I simply decree, in the name of Jesus Christ, that they take away triple of what they came to leave, so that they have something to scratch themselves with when they return home after coming to my events with delusions of being superheroes.

Furthermore, on one occasion, without me asking for any proof, my Lord Jesus Christ showed me the power that we priests have when we act with faith. I was performing a liberation for a young woman, around twenty-five years old, who was being targeted by her jealous neighbor with a witch- craft spell to kill her

24

through an anorexia curse. Exhausted from multiple sessions, as whatever I removed from the young woman returned without delay, I pleaded with God to unleash His wrath upon the woman who wished such harm upon that poor girl. I made this plea at three in the morning, worn out after a whole night of liberation prayers trying to break these curses. The next day, the girl's call interrupted my desired rest, but my sleepiness vanished when I learned that precisely at three in the morning, the neighbor across the street, the witch herself, at the very hour we had entrusted her to God's justice, had fallen asleep while driving and collided with a truck, tragically losing her life.

Please note that in our prayers we never wish harm upon anyone, as this is prohibited by the Gospel of Jesus Christ. Instead, we simply entrust the situation to God's just arm, for we saw that our strength was already at its limit, and only God could put an end to such wickedness.

I will cite several examples to illustrate what we just said: the first one is the case of a man who told me that he didn't believe in the devil, let alone in the power of witchcraft. He had believed in God as a child but had lost his faith over time. This man, after a life of moral disarray, fell into the hands of a superstitious woman who was very fond of consulting witches. He confessed to me that after ending the relationship with this woman, his life had taken a complete turn. From a situation of economic solvency that allowed him all his excesses in terms of alcohol and women, he saw each of his businesses go bankrupt. However, what brought him back to the search for God was when his health was seriously affected by illnesses that medically had no explanation. He assured that if it weren't for the diabolical intervention in his life, he wouldn't have returned to the bosom of the Church, seeking confession and sacramental life, understanding that God used hardships to see his prodigal children return.

The second example, unlike the previous one, is of people who believe they are immune because they lead an active spiritual life. The case is of a woman who came to see me because she had been experiencing a strange phenomenon for some time that she couldn't explain: while she was praying the rosary, she felt an uncontrollable anger that moved her to break it into pieces. When I told her that this was a symptom of diabolic infestation, the woman vehemently denied it, arguing that she went to Mass and prayed the rosary every day, that she sometimes even spent an entire night in vigil in front of the Blessed Sacrament, and confessed frequently. Therefore, being in a state of grace, the devil couldn't manifest through her.

I told her that if she wanted, I could perform a liberation prayer to see if there was something within her. The thing was, when I imposed a crucifix about ten inches tall on her forehead, the woman fell to the floor, writhing, her eyes rolling back and showing supernatural strength, so much so that without touching the crucifix, she broke it as if it exploded by itself. The head of Christ fell to one side, the crossbeam, and arms to another, and the rest of the body remained on the crossbeam I held in my hands. Note that the crucifix was solid metal.

When the woman came, I explained what had happened, but she did not believe my words and did not want to submit to the rest of the treatment. As my supreme rule is never to attempt to liberate someone who does not wish to be freed, sadly I had to let her go with her demon inside.

The last example I want to give is a warning to clerics who think that their priestly or episcopal vestments make them immune to witchcraft. I remember once when I arrived in Medellin to visit my parents, a group of laypeople who were helping a priest came to me to say that witchcraft had been injected into him through the housemaid, and at that moment he was in a coma with no hope for life, as the concoction had caused three strokes in the left cerebral lobe and two on the right.

They asked me, as an exorcist, to do them the favor of performing a liberation prayer for him because, according to the doctors, he would not make it through the night, and if he did, he would be bedridden. I immediately asked for a picture of the priest and started praying over it with faith, for even though I was in another city, the power of God could reach him through the photo, in the same way as witches analogously invoke the evil of Satan on a person through a photo.

The moment I started the prayer, I felt uncontrollable nausea, and I understood that the Lord was going to expel the witch's brew through me; after expelling transparent saliva and catching my breath by drinking a little exorcised water, I continued the liberation prayer until I felt completely restored. Two days later, the priest's assistants called me with the great news that not only had he come out of the coma, but he had already been discharged and was celebrating Mass at his home, perfectly restored and with no sequels from the strokes.

As you can see, being pious or consecrated as a priest or religious person does not grant diplomatic immunity from the forces of evil. God cannot reward a lack of faith, to believe that witchcraft is harmless is to distort the Word of God, that's why we will return to this topic later. As I mentioned earlier, many Catholics and especially priests think that not believing in witchcraft reduces its effectiveness, which is totally incorrect, for witchcraft obtains its strength from an act of faith in the power of evil, not from a psychological action. Therefore, saying that one does not believe in it neither protects nor diminishes its efficacy.

But before I finish, I must humbly confess that we don't always come out on top. On some occasions, illnesses have been inflicted on our ministry and on me, and the only solution has been to bear them with patience, offering them up for the conversion of our enemies. We know they are not natural diseases because it is inexplicable that everyone suffers from, for example, stomach problems at the same time, even those members of the ministry who have not been able to attend our meetings or who have been away in other cities, so we rule out the possibility of a virus contracted by working together.

Likewise, we sometimes suffer cuts on our body that appear from one day to the next while we sleep, or bruises as if we had been hit. On one occasion a hand mark appeared on my neck as if someone had tried to strangle me during the night. But in case anyone still doubts whether witchcraft is effective or ineffective, let's demonstrate it in the following chapter.

Chapter II

General Concepts

Most people who deny the effectiveness of witchcraft, in reality, hide their fears behind rationalism. Thus, it is a psychological self-defense to claim that witchcraft is a product of imagination and superstition, and that it is impossible for spells and magical potions to have any effect. This happens because they do not receive with faith the evidence that life gives us on the subject. To clarify the effectiveness of witchcraft, I am reminded of my first encounter with the destructive effects of the magical arts.

I was serving in a parish in the Vucetich neighborhood in Argentina when a young, desperate, crying mother approached me. She pleaded for me to take pity on her little boy, who was a year and a half old. He had a disease with which the doctors had grown tired of fighting, as they had applied all their knowledge and medicines without any results, and also, the disease was a dermal attack on his entire face, a crusting that covered his forehead, cheek, nose, and chin. Indeed, the boy looked monstrous due to the crusts that covered his face. The mother assured me that she had exhausted her resources visiting all dermatologists and specialists, but none had improved the situation with their treatments. Deep down, she knew it was not a bodily disease, but an affliction imposed by the arts of sorcery, but none of the doctors believed her, nor did the priests or the bishop. But she had decided to turn to me as a last resort, as she did not want to go to the witches, who she knew were not only causing harm to her boy but had also caused the loss of her husband. The strange thing about the case was that the decomposition of her boy's face occurred every month when she took him to visit his father's grave in the cemetery, which confirmed that the spiritual disease of the child was intergenerationally death hex that had sent his father to the grave.

I decided to believe the desperate mother and prayed with all my strength, laying my hands on the boy's face, which I had previously anointed with exorcised oil; as soon as I touched the boy's face, he writhed and screamed as if I were placing a red-hot iron on him. When the child calmed down, I ended my prayer. I told the mother to anoint his face with exorcised oil and to come see me the following week, in case a second deliverance prayer was needed.

My surprise and joy were indescribable when they presented me with a completely healthy child, so much so that I didn't even recognize him: his little face was clean, and his skin was rosy with a deep smile of gratitude. The boy's mother was deeply grateful and asked me what else was necessary to complete her son's deliverance process. I told her it was enough to continue anointing him for a few more days until his skin fully recovered, and that she should avoid under all circumstances letting her child step foot in a cemetery again.

It was then that I realized that hexes truly exist and that our prayers had the power to undo them. I will try to explain here where the efficacy of hexes comes from, starting with the efficacy of prayers: in all religions, it is certain that if certain invocations are made to God, he responds by granting what is asked. Therefore, anyone who believes that our actions and prayers are effectively contemplated and attended to by God must accept that in the same way, those who have Satan as their god will have to be heard by him when they invoke him with certain prayers and a certain satanic liturgy that we call witchcraft or sorcery.

I will give the example of the Catholic Church to which I belong. In it, the sacraments combine material elements such as pouring water, anointing with oil, etc., with prayers that are intended to produce sanctifying grace in the person who receives them. Analogously, a spell is the combination of actions with material elements, plus formulas of spiritual invocations, that are intended to achieve a malevolent effect on someone.

So, it's contradictory for those who believe in God and practice a religion, believing in the effectiveness of their liturgical acts and prayers, to deny the effectiveness of spells, because if we are going to be fair, we would have to accept both things.

Apart from this, I want to consider those who have em- braced faith in Christ, that if the practice of sorcery, spiritualism, and divination were harmless, then God would have made a mistake and even committed an injustice by condemning and punishing these practices so severely in the Sacred Scriptures.

DIFFERENCE BETWEEN MAGICIAN, SORCERER, WITCH, AND SHAMAN

The major problem we face is the lack of knowledge we all have about the esoteric and hidden world, as we have few reports that come directly from the source; that is, there are few high-level sorcerers who have converted and can tell us about the methods and doctrines that a person must acquire to officially call themselves a witch or sorcerer.

I think I should start by clarifying the great confusion that most people have between what a magician, a witch, a sorcerer, and a shaman are:

The magician

The magician is the man who dedicates himself to the pursuit of hidden knowledge and arcane wisdom, and seeks to develop methods of extracorporeal action through his mental powers or superhuman abilities. In the past, magicians were synonymous with

31

philosophers who sought wisdom in the stars and in the thoughts inherited from the oldest cultures, hence three magicians through their wisdom went to meet the promised Messiah as recorded in the Gospel.

Also, the term magician is used for those who have the ability to draw attention with their arts to distract and entertain, who should more appropriately be called prestidigitators. This word means quick fingers and alludes to quick hand movements that deceive the eyes and the attention of the viewers, creating the sensation that things appear and disappear. Or they could also be called illusionists, who with mirrors, curtains, or false bottoms create the sensation that a person can be split in half and other similar cases. From here, the practice of this type of magic does not go against either God or the Church and is harmless to people, as its only objective is to entertain.

However, if the magician in his search for hidden magic enters the realm of the diabolical, of course, he will be completely outside the law of God and therefore it will not be lawful for anyone to practice magic or seek such knowledge. In this case, instead of a magician, he should be called an occultist.

The witch

The witch doctor is a person who practices the art of causing certain things to happen by invoking the forces of nature, whose effects can be either beneficial or harmful. Normally, the witch uses the power of herbs and minerals to achieve their effects, they could also be called a herbalist.

In most cases, although the witch does not directly invoke Satan or make pacts with him, they do demand from nature effects that can only come from this evil being, as nature cannot produce such consequences. Therefore, the witch is in mortal sin because they deny the uniqueness of God: they attribute divinity to the forces of nature, which in other words would be pantheism.

I recall a case that came to my attention in Peru, of a poor woman who, finding herself afflicted with a pain in her belly, which turned out to be appendicitis according to the autopsy, not having the money to go to a health center, turned to the local healer. He supplied her with a potion in which he combined several typical herbs of the region and other elements that, although harmless separately, when combined became a deadly poison, especially since it was prepared with non-potable water. This increased the number of intestinal bacteria that caused peritonitis and led to the death of the unfortunate patient, who, believing in the witch, endured these indescribable pains in the hope that the magic potion would soon work, when in reality what came upon her was death.

It is sad to see how poor people, not having money for traditional medicine, turn to these witches looking for an alternative solution to their ailments, and due to the incompetence of these men, in most cases, the situation worsens if not ends tragically.

The shaman

He is the one who, making use of spiritual entities, tries to ward off diseases of the soul and body. Usually, to achieve their ends, they mix elements of witchcraft, magic, and sorcery, and we could more plainly call him a healer.

In these times, it has become very popular to resort to this type of indigenous witchcraft with the so-called Yagé, which I scarcely recommend, in fact, I consider it supremely dangerous in the spiritual field. For those who do not know what Yagé is, it is a drink extracted from an Amazonian plant of the same name, which is used in a ritual that seeks contact with the Spiritual. Rationalists argue that the plant is a hallucinogen that causes mystical delusions.

Yagé followers argue that this drink is not a barbiturate, but has the property of opening the soul to spiritual experiences and contacts.

My opinion as an exorcist is that whether it is a hallucinogen or a substance with spiritual powers, the ritual that accompanies the intake of Yagé, plus the ingestion of the substance, certainly alarmingly lowers levels of consciousness and makes the person open to the influence of spiritual entities of all kinds. Among the people I have had to attend to after having ingested Yagé, I have found demonic possession with souls of shamans that manifest within them or suffering souls that have been put into them thanks to the ritual and the low levels of consciousness to which they exposed themselves imprudently.

Apart from the danger of becoming possessed, we must also consider that there are psychological diseases that have worsened or that have developed because of these experiences with Yagé. Therefore, I strongly recommend that everyone refrain from such pagan rituals, which although normally accompanied by indigenous Catholic chants, remnants left over from the catechism of missionaries, are by no means the center, nor the goal of the ritual, as it dates from long before Christian evangelization and therefore its goal is to enter into a spiritual dimension infested with pagan deities. All its original elements belong to spiritualism, witchcraft, and idolatry, typical of superstitions inherent in indigenous culture.

I should also add something about "civilized" shamans who offer their services in big cities, usually these belong more to the field of sorcery and are conscienceless men who have no limits when it comes to deceiving the unsuspecting to take their money. I have already come across several cases of women to whom the shaman has said that the only way to rid themselves of the curse that afflicts them is to have sexual relations with him, and the sad thing is that the poor ignorant women fall into these traps, risking not only contracting venereal diseases, but also acquiring sexual contamination and influence from these men that leaves them

34

"bewitched", as it is commonly said, thus becoming their sexual playthings. Even mothers subject their daughters to herbal baths,

Where these innocent creatures have to pose naked under the lewd gaze of the one who is performing the sprinkling.

The power these people can have with their potions is so terrible, that I recall the case of a young girl who came to me in despair because of what had happened to her. The girl lived with her father and an older brother, and one day was surprised when the building doorman asked her how many boyfriends she had. She indignantly told him that she had never had a boyfriend and much less did they visit her there where her father and brother were. The matter rested there, until the girl began to feel that something strange was happening to her because she had manifestations of demonic possession at a healing mass she had attended.

Worried, she sought out a prayer group in the parish, there she befriended a young man who had recently converted from a life of much sin and who during the meetings could not stop looking at her in amazement. When she asked the young man why he looked at her like that, he told her he was very glad that she had also converted from a life of so much sin. She didn't know what he was talking about and he told her that if she was on the path of conversion she should not be ashamed of having been a prostitute. She was indignant, as she had never sold herself to any man. The young man insisted saying that he himself had hired her and had sex with her on more than three occasions, that her own father and brother were the ones who charged for sleeping with her and that indeed the lust with which she performed her work was more worthy of a demon than of an ordinary woman.

In light of the young man's sincere claims, the girl began to investigate and was devastated by the evidence she found: her father and brother were high-level shamans, and through their potions, they had caused her to be possessed by lustful spirits, which made her lose consciousness and allowed them to sell her as a sexual object. With this discovery, she finally understood the reason why she frequently experienced vaginal bleeding and numbness in her entire reproductive system. Although we were able to achieve her complete liberation, we could never make her complete her process of inner healing because she always maintained that she could never forgive her father and brother for such a despicable act.

The Sorcerer

The sorcerer is the person who dedicates themselves to the evocation of negative or malevolent forces through potions, spells, and enchantments in order to achieve beneficial or, in most cases, harmful effects on another person. Unlike the witch who works with elements of nature, the sorcerer requires an object of contact with their victim; something that belongs to them, such as hair, clothing, jewelry, and so on.

It goes without saying that the practice of sorcery is a grave sin against God's law, as we are forbidden to wish harm upon our neighbor, and the sorcerer is a professional of malevolence who not only wishes harm but also causes it.

For those who are beginning to open their hearts to the realities we are trying to warn about in this book, I want to share a story that illustrates the spiritual power that these agents of evil can exert from a distance, with the sole purpose of making their victims suffer.

The case involves a woman who was brought to me from a city that was 150 kilometers away from where I was attending. She had been bedridden for two years, unable to care for her family, with indescribable pain along her entire back and waist that prevented her from walking and even sleeping. Doctors, after conducting X-rays and detailed studies, had determined that there was no physical reason for her suffering, so all they could do was prescribe strong painkillers and send her home, where she had to writh in pain without any relief, as the medications had no effect.

When this woman heard that there was a priest who prayed for people afflicted by witchcraft, she arranged to be transported to my chapel amidst tears and screams of pain. When she stood before me, I immediately realized that she was under a voodoo curse, performed through a transfer spell. These types of spells involve burying the hair, photo, or a piece of clothing belonging to the person one wants to harm inside a wax doll. It is called a transfer spell because the pain and damage inflicted on the doll with pricks or burns are transferred to the victim.

I asked the woman if she believed that the Lord could free her from her suffering through me, and she replied that she was certain it would happen, which is why she had endured the ordeal of being transported to me. I asked her to indicate the areas where she felt pain, and in the name of Jesus Christ, I proceeded to spiritually remove the pins, although she couldn't see them, she knew that the pins were there, stuck in her. When I finished, the woman was crying, not from pain anymore, but out of gratitude and joy because she had regained her mobility. She could jump and walk freely.

The woman told me that she had nothing with which to repay me for such a favor. I replied that she didn't need to give me money, but I would ask her for something to convince her skeptical companions who were waiting outside, doubting that she would achieve healing. I asked her to sweep and mop the parish office. I still remember the astonished faces of the four people who came with her when I let them in and saw her with a broom in hand, moving furniture and sweeping as if she had never experienced any pain. They couldn't believe it. They had to carry her among the four of them, and she would cry out in pain every moment, needing to take a painkiller.

As we can see, the power of sorcerers is quite strong, and unfortunately, due to the lack of a cohesive force within the Catholic

Church that confronts their actions, they freely exercise their wickedness, and their arrogance grows day by day. The victims have no choice but to suffer in silence, misunderstood by those who have been bestowed by Christ with the power and strength to undo the works of the devil and his agents.

Are they all bad?

As we have seen, neither occult magicians, nor shamans, nor sorcerers, nor even witches who claim not to invoke Satan to practice their arts,

They cannot claim to be completely innocent of the tragic effects their actions have on others. All of them deviate from the path of faith in the one true God and even trivialize His worship, leading people to believe that they can manipulate and control divinity through certain formulas or procedures. That is why Sacred Scripture prohibits us from seeking their help and invites us to trust in God, who will not fail to provide for our needs if we ask with humility.

The only thing we could accept is that some of them, when they first entered these paths, did so out of ignorance and without malice, but over time, they must inevitably realize that their arts, sooner or later, cause harm.

DIFFERENCE BETWEEN SPELL, INCANTATION, AND ENCHANTMENT.

To delve a little deeper into the topic we have been discussing, I want to briefly discuss these three elements commonly used in magical arts, as understanding how evil works will make it easier for us to undo its effects through spiritual action and true Catholic faith that opposes its power.

SPELL

It is a procedure that combines physical elements such as hair, clothing, photographs, etc., of the person one wants to affect, with the recitation of certain magical formulas.

The spell is performed with the aim of breaking the restrictions that God has placed on Satan, allowing him to act against that person.

To give an example of a spell, I'll share the case of a young woman who approached me saying that she felt stuck, without the desire to continue living, and that her heart had dried up. Her social and economic life were not progressing, and she suspected that people who envied her had cast a spell on her to reduce her to that state. A priest who is not knowledgeable in these matters would have simply advised the young woman not to think badly of others, to ignore those negative thoughts, and to entrust everything to God and move forward in the daily struggle. Personally, I'm not one to take the easy path because from my experience, I know that Satan often hides himself so that we cannot detect his presence and thus he can freely torture our sheep. Therefore, I decided to pray for her deliverance to see what the Lord would reveal. As soon as I began to pray, the girl collapsed on the floor and her vital signs dramatically decreased, to the point where I had to interrupt the prayer and revive her, bringing her out of the trance.

Based on her reaction just by laying hands on her, I was certain that it was witchcraft, but I needed more information to determine the source of the hex. She then mentioned that the only thing she had omitted was that since her life began to stagnate, she had also developed a deep fear of entering her own business. I asked her what her profession was, and she told me that she owned an ice cream shop, which gave me a clue about the source of her problem.

Among the Umbandas, who are a Afro-Brazilian sect of satanic Santeria, the spell of "frizamiento" or freezing is very common. It involves writing the name of the person whom harm is intended on a piece of paper, and then pinning it with needles onto a piece of meat that is subsequently placed in a freezer. This spell freezes the person's economic, emotional, and vital aspects.

Once we discovered the source of that poor woman's afflictions, we proceeded to perform her deliverance. During the process, the girl's body temperature, while in a trance, dropped alarmingly as if she were physically frozen. We invoked the fire of the Holy Spirit and rubbed her body as one would do to someone in an attempt to restore their vital warmth during hypothermia. Thank God, after half an hour of anguished prayer, we managed to restore her vital signs along with her desire to live, fight, love, and serve God.

The Spell

It is the use of a formula with which one hopes to achieve a physical or spiritual effect through the mediation of evil forces, without the need for any additional procedure or action. One of the spells I have frequently encountered is the one that invokes incubus or succubus demons. The existence of these demons dates back to the Middle Ages, and they have the ability to touch people and even engage in a kind of sexual act with those who are oppressed by them. In the case of women, it is the incubi who perpetrate the assault, which in some instances can be vaginal and In the case of men, which is less frequent, they are called succubi because they exert a certain suction on the male sexual organ.

I know that in this modern century, many people think what I used to think until these types of cases started coming to me: that women in the Middle Ages blamed demons for losing their virginity. But in this modern world, where women don't care about losing their purity, if they talk about being sexually harassed by a spirit, it's because there is a reality behind it.

Here, I want to mention the case of a young woman in her mid-twenties who came to me with the warning that when she told me what was happening to her, I would think she was crazy, but it didn't bother her as she had even asked her sister to have her admitted to a psychiatric hospital. She told me that a young man from the neighborhood, who belonged to the satanic sect of the Umbandas, had tried to court her and proposed that she sleep with him. When the young woman told him that she was Catholic and that she wouldn't engage in such acts, especially knowing what sect he belonged to, he threatened her, saying she would regret it when "someone else" slept with her.

From that moment on, every night at three in the morning, the door of her room would open and she would feel a spiritual entity getting on her bed, causing the mattress to sink where it rested. Then, it would grab her arms tightly and open her legs to sexually violate her, feeling a cold gust of wind inside her when that creature completed its sexual act.

I knew she wasn't crazy because of the information I had about incubus demons. I confessed to her that initially, I believed it was an invention of women in the Middle Ages, but I had changed my opinion based on the testimonies of many contemporary women who had no shame in admitting they had lost their virginity.

The process for this girl, although challenging, culminated in the complete liberation from such diabolical oppressions. We had to perform several sessions of exorcism and claim her sexual freedom in the name of Jesus Christ, with her renouncing all previous sins of the flesh and breaking any pact her mother or ancestors may have made with forces of evil. She recalled that her mother regularly sought out witches, even spending sleepless nights praying to God in her final days for protection against everything that had been unleashed upon her, which caused her daughter to develop the ability to feel and see spiritual entities.

If someone asked me for a theological explanation of how these things are possible, I would refer to passages in the Holy Scriptures that state certain angels have the power to have physical contact with a human being, although certainly not in a sexual manner. For example, we see how Jacob physically wrestled with an angel all night, in a way so real that the angel injured one of Jacob's thigh tendons. Likewise, we see Saint Raphael interact with Tobias in the Book of Tobit, tangible and perceptible like any ordinary human being.

Those texts demonstrate that an angel can have physical contact with a human being if God allows it, and obviously, if good angels can do it, the evil ones can as well, as seen on numerous occasions in the lives of saints who have suffered diabolical harassments.

The enchantment or sorcery

It is the action by which one attempts to predict the future based on the interpretation of present events, such as cartomancy or palmistry, reading the palm of the hand, coffee readings, and so on. Many people believe that consulting these arts is harmless, but if God condemns it so strictly in His Holy Scripture, it is not because it is a harmless falsehood, but because He knows it is one of the snares by which Satan traps many unsuspecting individuals.

Knowing the future is something that fascinates humans, and many start by reading horoscopes out of mere curiosity. But when they see that the things predicted there start to come true little by little, they end up in such slavery that they cannot make a decision in their lives without consulting a fortune-teller, which is not what God wants for His children. What is truly terrible is that as children of God, we are completely free, and our future directly depends on God's will. That is why we will be freer the more we live by the motto of the Virgin Mary: "Let it be done to me according to your will." But when a child of God allows themselves to be seduced by Satan, mysteriously, their future becomes detached from God's will and becomes subject to the arbitrary and oppressive will of Satan.

Hence, it is not that Satan knows all futures, but rather that he can know and, to some extent, determine the futures of those individuals who have consecrated themselves to him through their acts of faithlessness towards God and their reliance on divinatory arts.

In the Bible, we can find repeated warnings regarding this matter, and we can realize that the future can indeed be known, but the source for knowing the future that only God knows is not the fortune-tellers but the prophets sent by Him.

It is also important to consider that there are futures that can be known directly by God's creatures. For example, humans have developed the ability to interpret astrophysical movements and predict events such as the passage of a comet, planetary cycles, or stellar collisions.

There are other futures knowable to angels, such as certain reactions that some individuals may have in the face of difficulties, certain natural catastrophes like earthquakes, or certain diseases that will develop, which may be imperceptible to human instruments but fall within the scope of angelic perspective.

But there are other futures that are only knowable to God. These are the free futures that depend on human freedom, which is in constant motion since each new circumstance opens up a range of infinite possibilities that only God can decipher and know their ultimate consequences even before the person comes into existence. Therefore, Satan, through divination, seeks to restrict as much as possible the exercise of free decision-making by his followers.

This allows him to calculate probabilities in order to more accurately predict the future that he himself is conditioning with his continuous predictions.

Hexes

A hex is a spiritual action that, although sometimes accompanied by material elements, always seeks to bring harm to a person. As I previously explained, a hex derives its power from an act of faith that a human being places in the forces of evil, attempting to unleash them against the intended target. We have also seen that hexes are crafted through a spell or incantation, but here we want to warn about certain ways in which hexes are delivered and how we should undo them.

One of the most common methods of delivering hexes to individuals is by introducing them into preferred dark beverages such as coffee or dark sodas, or in foods that are known to be our taste and preference. Although we shouldn't become overly sensitive when receiving gifted food, if we have clear evidence that consuming a specific food consistently brought by the same person results in a relapse of a frequent illness, for which doctors cannot provide an explanation, or if we experience an increase in temptations or emotional states that undermine our faith or physical health, it is advisable to be cautious. In fact, I don't even recommend refusing to accept food, as the person bringing it may suspect that we have become aware of their intentions, they will change tactics and attack us in a worse way. The best course of action is to always accept the food but not consume it, instead, give it to someone else, as hexes are usually specifically made with a specific first and last name and may not affect someone for whom it was not intended.

I recall the case of a man involved in politics to whom I gave this advice. He hadn't asked for my advice on the matter, but since there is a lot of witchcraft in the field of politics, I thought it was better to be cautious. Later, he confessed that he was surprised when, days after my warning, a lady appeared with a banana cake. When he thanked her and said he would eat it later, she insisted that she wouldn't leave until he ate it. The more he insisted that he didn't want to consume it at that moment, the more she insisted that he shouldn't reject it since she had made it with love. Finally, the woman had to accept the politician's position, and as she was leaving, she told the bodyguards to make sure he ate it.

Obviously, once the lady left the house, the politician had the cake thrown in the trash, thinking he had gotten rid of it. However, he was surprised when the woman appeared days later, accusing him of not having eaten the cake, and even though he assured her that he had, she insisted that she knew he was lying.

As you can see, it doesn't take much suspicion to realize the ill intentions with which they were giving the cake to the politician, you see, that woman can't assert with certainty that she knew he hadn't eaten the cake unless she was expecting a negative effect on his life or health.

Certainly, there can be cases where the curse placed on food is so harmful that it can affect people for whom the harm was not intended. For example, I remember that an exorcist's wine for consecration was conjured. He became aware of it because one of his assistants was secretly drinking it. The young woman started developing a rash on her face and felt unbearable itching after her pious thefts. When she noticed that she had developed a gastrointestinal illness similar to what the exorcist priest had been suffering from for a while, she decided to confess her crime and ask him to break the conjure affecting the sacramental wine, as it had caused the illness in both him and the pious thief. Sometimes God uses the weaknesses of a priest's servants to expose the dangerous evil conjured, even in an element that had to be used by him.

Since we are discussing conjures, I must warn people who come across the elements used in the spell to be careful when getting rid of them, as they can have secondary effects on the person handling them. Let me share a case that happened to me while I was in the United States, during a trip to give some lectures.

After one of my talks, a woman approached me and told me that she was very frightened because, out of ignorance, she had performed a spell following the instructions of a witch, desperate because her partner was being unfaithful. She was afraid that undoing the spell would unleash harm in her home, so she asked me for help.

I obviously asked her for more details, and she told me that the witch had told her that part of the ritual had to be performed by him in Mexico, using her partner's underwear, while the other part had to be done by her using the elements he would indicate.

The witch instructed her to take a chili pepper, representing her partner's genitalia, insert a photo of her partner into it, tie it with a red ribbon, making seven knots, and then bury it in a flowerpot in her garden. According to esoteric tradition, the seven knots represent the seven chakras of the soul that govern the powers and senses of the human being. Therefore, making these seven knots symbolizes binding the whole person to the one they want to control, seeking to spiritually incapacitate them from thinking, looking, or desiring any other woman in this case.

When I told the woman that the way to break the curse was by unearthing it from the flowerpot and throwing it into a river, she expressed fear of the satanic fury that could be unleashed by doing so. She insisted so much that I had to agree to do that task myself. The next day, the woman showed up with the hanging flowerpot in a garbage bag, just as I had requested to avoid direct contact with the item. As several exorcists have stated, touching this type of burial directly with bare hands can lead to lifelong spiritual and physical illnesses for the exorcist.

I asked two of my assistants to take me to a nearby river to dispose of the soil and break the curse. But coincidentally, as soon as we set off, torrential rain started pouring, making it difficult for us to move forward.

If anyone thinks it could have been a coincidence and not a satanic intervention to prevent us from undoing their work, the driver informed me that the brakes had mysteriously stopped working, and therefore we couldn't move forward as she was losing control of the car. Since I don't believe in coincidences, I proceeded to exorcise the car's brakes. As soon as I finished the prayer, they started working again, and the rain stayed behind. We were able to reach the river and get out of the car without a single drop falling on us.

At the riverbank, I anointed my hands with exorcised oil, then covered them with plastic bags to avoid direct contact with the soil. I also sprinkled the soil with exorcised water and salt before I began digging in the flowerpot. When I found what was left of the chili pepper and the red string, which had been buried there for years, I broke the bindings, and a putrid smell was released, which was illogical as the dried seasoning shouldn't have smelled like anything but earth.

The spiritual contamination that was unleashed had such an impact on us that all three of us had to retreat, gagging without being able to vomit anything, and feeling a burning sensation on our faces as if acid had been poured on us. My hands were also affected by irritation, which only returned to normal after weeks of anointing them with exorcised oil and washing them with exorcised water. Therefore, I warn that some witchcraft can affect us even when protected with gloves or anointed with exorcised oil, but it's a price to pay for the liberation of souls.

After taking a breath, we resumed our task until we managed to throw that spell into the river, asking the Lord to let the waters of that river, symbolizing the Holy Spirit and flowing from the altar of God, undo the works of Satan and the power given to him through that spell we were casting into them.

I want to emphasize that when faced with conjure, the effectiveness of us breaking it depends directly on the level of our faith. If the faith the sorcerer has in Satan is greater than the faith the Catholic affected by the conjure has in Jesus Christ, the breaking performed by the praying person may not have full efficacy or at least not as desired. This should in no way be interpreted as the prince of this world has more power than Jesus Christ, but rather that the almighty strength of our God is limited by the low faith of the person seeking liberation from maleficent oppression.

The effectiveness of a breaking we want to perform is not found in the length and detail of our prayers, but in the intensity of our act of faith in the power of God when we recite them. As Our Lord Jesus Christ said (Matthew 6:7) we don't need to multiply words to be heard in our prayers, but rather we should limit them to what is necessary to move the heart of our God. Therefore, we suggest focusing more on multiplying acts of love for God and trust in Him, rather than prayers of repulsion against infernal forces.

Furthermore, I would dare to say that the most effective action against any hex or diabolical incursion in our lives is the frequent use of the sacraments of the Catholic Church, especially confession and communion, combined with the daily recitation of the Holy Rosary. For, as we should all know, the more presence of Christ and Mary there is in our lives, the fewer satanic influences there will be, as they are inversely proportional.

However, many people, by multiplying the intentions for which they offer Mass and the Rosary, diminish their effectiveness because their act of faith is not strong enough to address such a diversity of objectives. Therefore, I recommend that individuals who feel affected by hexes concentrate on offering the Holy Mass and the Rosary solely and exclusively for the breaking of the evils that have been conjured upon them.

To conclude these notions, I will describe how individuals who, through divine inspiration, come across any witchcraft performed with the elements described here or in subsequent chapters, should proceed.

RECOMMENDED PROCEDURES FOR UNDOING ENCOUNTERED WITCHCRAFT

When the elements found are susceptible to burning, such as wood, fabrics, wax dolls, photos, etc., they should be taken to an open field, avoiding physical contact with them.

There, you should sprinkle them with a flammable substance, preferably gasoline or alcohol, with great care to prevent any fire from spreading; Satan is very vengeful, and it is necessary to take all possible precautions, including having a fire extinguisher nearby. While the elements burn in the fire, you shall recite the following prayer or a similar one inspired by the Lord:

Deign, Almighty God, to bless this fire, so that it may be a symbol of the presence of the Holy Spirit and the living flame of love that burns in the Sacred Heart of Jesus, the Immaculate Heart of Mary, and the Chaste Heart of St. Joseph. By destroying these physical elements, may all spiritual and bodily evils conjured against your beloved children through them also be annihilated. May all curses of death, disease, or ruin, symbolized by the elements that we submit under the power of your flame of love, be dissolved. May this be done in the name of God the Almighty Father, God the Redeemer of the World, God the Holy Spirit, with the power to bind and loose entrusted to the Holy Catholic Church, through the intercession of the Blessed Virgin Mary and the ministry of the Holy Archangels Michael, Gabriel, and Raphael. Amen.

When the found items cannot be burned, such as metals, porcelain, stone, bone, etc., then they should be transported to a location with running water, either a river or the sea, or alternatively any stream or brook with sufficient flow to carry away the discarded items, in order to prevent someone else from finding them and taking them home. When disposing of these items in the water, the following prayer should be recited:

> *Almighty God, deign to bless this water, making it a symbol of the presence of the Holy Spirit and the eternal springs that flow from the Throne of God and the Lamb. May it carry away all physical and spiritual evils that have been conjured against your beloved children through these objects. May all curses of death, illness, or ruin be dissolved, symbolized by the elements we submit to the power of the river of living water. Let this be done in the name of God the Almighty Father, God the Redeemer Son of the World, and God the Holy Spirit, with the power to bind and loosen that the Holy Mother Church possesses, through the intercession of the Most Holy Virgin Mary and the ministry of the Archangels Saint Michael, Saint Gabriel, and Saint Raphael. Amen.*

As we have been discussing throughout the book about the use of sacramentals, and surely many people are interested in having them, we will include here some prayers so that when you bring water, salt, and oil to a priest, you can present them to him for him to proceed with their blessing.

Blessings

Blessing of the Water

> *Dignify yourself, Almighty Lord, to bless this water, symbol of the Grace of the Holy Spirit received in baptism, through which we were freed from the chains of Satan and sin, and imprint upon it the power to repel the snares of the devil, the world, and the flesh, giving it the power to cast out demons, dissolve hexes, and for the souls who receive it to regain their spiritual and physical health.*

And may this blessing be carried out in the name of Almighty God the Father, God the Son, Redeemer of the World, and God the Holy Spirit, with the power to bind and loose that the Holy Catholic Church possesses, through the intercession of the Blessed Virgin Mary and the ministry of the Holy Archangels Michael, Gabriel, and Raphael. Amen.

Blessing of the oil

Almighty God, deign to bless this oil, a symbol of the anointing of the Holy Spirit, which has been used since the Old Testament to anoint kings, prophets, and priests. Grant it the power to heal the spiritual wounds of your children who daily face Satan and his followers. Wherever this oil is applied, may all entrances be closed to the creatures of darkness, may all chains of satanic oppression be broken, and may all diseases resulting from the bite of the ancient serpent be healed. May your beloved children, anointed by your love, be free from the yoke of Satan. And may this blessing be poured out in the name of Almighty God the Father, Redeemer of the World, Holy Spirit, with the power to bind and loose as possessed by the Holy Mother Church, through the intercession of the Blessed Virgin Mary and the ministry of the Holy Archangels, St. Michael, St. Gabriel, and St. Raphael. Amen.

Blessing of salt

God of Power and Majesty, we beseech you to bless this salt, symbol of the grace you have poured upon Christians who have been placed in the world to prevent the corruption of Satan, and elevate the natural property of this salt to prevent the decay of the flesh to a spiritual level that prevents all

51

corruption originating from sin or instigations of the devil, the world, and passions, so that wherever it is placed, the presence of the devil and his cohorts cannot be. May all bindings of hexes be dissolved, and may those who receive it regain spiritual and physical health. And may this blessing be done in the name of God the Almighty Father, God the Redeemer of the World, God the Holy Spirit, with the power to bind and loose that the Holy Mother Church possesses, through the intercession of the Blessed Virgin Mary and the ministry of the Holy Archangels, Saint Michael, Saint Gabriel, and Saint Raphael. Amen.

Once we have assimilated the basic concepts used in the esoteric realm and illuminated them with some examples of how they manifest in reality, let us now delve into the subject by examining, one by one, the different types of magic that exist in the market.

I would like to clarify that I do not aim to exhaust the entire subject for two reasons: firstly, because we want to avoid turning this book into a manual of witchcraft that, instead of preventing and stopping its influence, leads the unwary to investigate and practice it. Secondly, because the malice and creativity of the forces of the underworld never sleep or rest, they will always be devising new ways to deceive the unsuspecting and harm the children of God.

Chapter III
White Magic

In this chapter, we will begin a journey through the different types of magic, or rather witchcraft, which can affect us. As we saw in the previous chapter, if we are going to talk about magic, we should refer to it as esoteric or occult magic rather than just magic. However, I will continue using the term "magic" because it is the most commonly used term to describe the study and manipulation of hidden forces.

I also want to clarify the use of colors to categorize the different types of magic. Depending on the witchcraft tradition, the interpretations of colors can vary greatly. For example, some may consider yellow magic to be associated with prosperity because the color represents gold, while others may associate it with gray magic, which encompasses economic matters. In this book, we will classify it as green magic. I want to emphasize that magic, in its general meaning, is the art that aims to produce certain events or effects at a distance.

Contrary to the laws of physics or the normal behavior of people, using the intervention of supernatural beings. Therefore, the subdivision we are going to make by colors is simply an attempt to divide the objectives sought with each type of magic, but they will always intermix because the spiritual realm is interconnected in a complex way. For example, if a person wanted to gain the love of a wealthy man to improve their economic status, they would need to utilize elements of red magic, which deals with love, green magic, which seeks prosperity, and blue magic, which employs mental control. By combining these three forces, they could attain the love of the man as well as control over his wealth.

All the types of magic we will see in the following chapters are actually one and the same magic. The division by colors is only meant to facilitate the differentiation of the procedures and objectives of each one. With this clarified, let us now delve into our first subdivision of magic, which is the topic of this chapter.

White magic is often referred to as benevolent magic because it does not seek to cause harm. In reality, this term is more of a modern invention, coined to contrast it with black magic as if it were its antagonist, seeking approval within Christian society.

White magic is a deception for unsuspecting Christians who believe that practicing it is akin to a venial sin or even something permitted by God's law. That is why those who practice white magic often hide behind Christian symbolism, such as that of saints and they also use elements very similar to the sacramentals of the Catholic Church, such as incense, water, salt, and oils... thus disguising the esoteric and even diabolical undertones. The major problem is, who do they seek the benefit from? As we saw earlier, if God condemns the practice of these arts, He will not act favorably if one were to ask for favors in a way that He Himself prohibits and condemns. That is why I must denounce that the benefits for which white magic intercedes are actually sought from Satan, and hence its effects cannot be lasting but will remain only as long as this malevolent deeming them useful in maintaining the state of the sin of the soul that practices or resorts to such magic.

To engage in these practices despite being a Christian is like lighting a candle to both God and the Devil. Unfortunately, the number of Catholics who play this double game and hypocritically try to reconcile with both forces, that of God and that of Satan, is incalculable.

The consequences of resorting to this type of magic go far beyond the person who unknowingly delves into these paths, as it affects their children and the children of their children for three or four generations, as stated in Exodus 20:5 in the Bible. Therefore, I recommend to readers who, out of ignorance or being influenced by others, have resorted to any kind of magic, to frequently pray the Prayer of Renunciation of Witchcraft at the end of this chapter, with the intention of snatching the power granted to Satan away from him. He has been given access to your life, your finances by tainting the money spent on agents of Satan, and to your future descendants.

The evil one has great power to divert your children, grandchildren, and great-grandchildren from the path of truth.

VARIETIES OF WHITE MAGIC

As white magic seeks to improve the quality of life by appealing to spiritual beings that protect or guide individuals in their decision-making, we will find the following arts camouflaged under the label of white magic in the market:

Santeria

This type of magic seeks to subjugate or manipulate Catholic saints in order to compel them to grant the most implausible whims of individuals, even contrary to the will of God. Among many other examples, we can mention the superstitious devotions that have spread to Saint Martha, Saint Helena, and the Virgin of "Untying Knots," especially the latter, which is regarded as a consecrated advocacy against witchcraft. It is also very common to invoke saints whose names are mixed with other unfamiliar ones, in such a way that they resemble a saint from the Catholic Church, but with that additional appellation indicating their falsification in Santeria, for example: Saint John the Miner, Saint John of the Street, Saint Mark of Leon, Saint Salvador of Horta, Saint Agnes of Monte Perdido, and so on.

Many people are unaware of the consequences that can arise from buying religious images from street vendors without knowing their origin or the faith of the business owners. I specifically recall the case of a fifteen-year-old girl in Argentina who bought a gold rosary from a vendor. She also saw images of San La Muerte, Gauchito Gil, and others, but didn't pay much attention to them. As soon as she put on the rosary, she immediately entered a trance and doesn't remember anything that happened, but her parents claim that she had tried to bite both of them and even attempted to strangle her younger brother. To free her from that state, they had to undergo a long process of deliverance until they managed to rid themselves of the acquired diabolical oppression.

Spiritism

This type of magic seeks to have contact with spiritual entities to assist in decision-making, know the future, or consult them about who is causing us harm or wishing us ill.

Spiritism is one of the major sources of diabolical possession, especially in people who serve as mediums (individuals who lend their bodies for the consulted spirit to manifest through their speech or gestures) or through the Ouija board (a board with letters, numbers, and the words "yes" and "no" used to communicate with the deceased, who move a pointer towards the letters to provide answers). The danger of these practices lies in the fact that most of the time it is the demons themselves who impersonate the invoked deceased entity, and through their responses, they make pronouncements or pacts that allow them to enter the bodies of unwary spiritualists; causing diabolical possession or oppression (satanic manifestations through words and gestures of a person in whom a demon habitually resides – possession – or in which it makes sporadic incursions – oppression).

Another excess of spiritism is inviting people to invoke historical or fictional characters, whom they portray with an appearance of holiness, creating esoteric and superstitious rituals around them in search of miraculous manifestations by these pseudo-saints. The most common spiritist cults in Latin America include José Gregorio Hernández, Negro Felipe, María Leoncia, Gauchito Gil, Pancho Sierra, San La Muerte, Don Juan de la Conquista, María de la Cabeza, Don Juan de los Caminos, Don Juan del Dinero, among many others. These figures are attributed with healing and miraculous powers that eventually reveal themselves as diabolical actions. To be freed from the side effects they produce, the intervention of an exorcist is necessary.

In my experience as an exorcist priest, I have had to attend to many young people who got involved in spiritism through the Ouija board; they even used it to predict the questions they would be asked in school exams. This addiction reached such extremes that even the demons determined who should have sexual relations with whom and whether they should marry or live in concubinage. As they tried to break free from it and start a life of conversion and prayer, symptoms of diabolical possession appeared. Without needing the board anymore, the demons spoke through them, even conjuring harm against the families of those affected.

After asking the young people to renounce witchcraft, especially spiritism, and to promise under oath not to consult spirits again, under the risk of being seven times more possessed than before, as Jesus states in Luke 11:24-ss, where he says that if a person from whom an exorcism has been performed returns to the same previous sins, the spirits that left him will return with seven even worse, and the situation will be worse in the end. After these warnings, we proceeded with their deliverance. The spirits explicitly stated that they did not want to leave because the young people had permitted them to possess them by practicing divination through the board. However, we argued that in the presence of Jesus

Christ himself, they had renounced this pact and claimed their freedom through our ministry, to which these condemned souls and demons could not resist and had to leave.

To see the satanic power that the Ouija board has, I also had to attend to a woman who had experienced a strong demonic infestation without ever consulting the board. How- ever, as the Lord showed us that the origin of this infestation was related to the use of the board, we asked the woman's niece, who also showed clear signs. This young girl confessed that she had acquired the demonic infestation by mocking her aunt because she thought that the fainting spells and the things she said were due to her being crazy. But when she started experiencing the same things, she became convinced that it was a spiritual reality. While they were praying for her deliverance, the unclean spirits showed them that enemies of their aunt had used the board to conjure demons upon her. Once the situation was clarified, I told the little girl that I wouldn't perform an exorcism on her because what she had was allowed by God to punish her pride and disbelief. I advised her to pray for her aunt, as once her aunt was set free, she would also be liberated from that oppression.

Just as I told the young girl, it happened exactly as I said. Once her aunt was liberated, she also returned to normal. This teaches us that we should have consideration and modesty regarding the spiritual sufferings of our brothers and sisters. If we mock their spiritual ailments, we may cause God to allow the intrusion of hell into our lives, so that we may become more charitable and aware of the spiritual support that these individuals need.

Divination

It is another malignant art that disguises itself under the label of white magic, seeking to know the future of individuals through various means. Many people have ruined their finances by spending large sums of money on astrology charts, tarot readings, or numerology. They have incurred such a curse in the economic realm that led them to ruin.

There are individuals who go to such extremes that they choose their wedding date based on the month in which they will have their astrology chart done, believing that it will determine whether their marriage will be successful or not. This leads to God not looking favorably upon a relationship built on superstition.

This also has the collateral effect of causing the children of such marriages to contract illnesses, be very rebellious, or have spiritual abnormalities.

Divination has many subdivisions, and among the most important ones, we find the following.

Astrology

It seeks to predict the future based on the position of the stars or celestial bodies, which are mistakenly believed to emit cosmic energies that affect the actions and thoughts of human beings. Within this type of divination, the most popular are horoscopes and astrology birth charts, both of which are very similar. The first consists of vague and general writings that attempt to forecast future events for individuals belonging to a specific zodiac sign based on their date of birth. The deception of this type of divination lies in the ambiguity of the predictions, which are so general and common in people's lives that they are bound to occur. The great danger arises when individuals become addicted to consulting horoscopes, relying on them for every decision, thus losing their freedom as children of God and becoming chained to this superstitious habit.

The second is a more sophisticated way of referring to the horoscope and is elaborated with a seemingly more scientific approach. It interprets the influence that the positions of the sun, moon, and planets have in relation to the celestial sphere and the horizon of a person's place of birth at the time of their birth. These positions are believed to influence, condition, and determine the personal and social characteristics of one's life. However, in many cases, astronomers have written extensively to debunk astrology as a science because if it were true, all people born on the same day and in the same place would have to experience the same events, which is never the case in reality, even for identical twins. Therefore, it is a serious mistake to place trust in such practices, especially considering the exorbitant sums of money charged for their elaboration.

Numerology

Is the discipline that studies the energetic vibration of numbers, attributing qualities to them beyond mathematics. Numbers are endowed with almost a personality of their own and a mystical influence, which supposedly has a transcendental impact on the personality, societies, projects, pets, and objects of specific individuals. Many unsuspecting individuals are lured by the scientific appearance of numerology and allow their lives to be manipulated by numbers associated with their date of birth, identification documents, residential addresses, and so on. In doing so, they lose the freedom that God desires for His children and attract divine curses for those who transgress the law of God.

Divination

When people surrender to superstition and indulge in the morbid pursuit of the future, they embrace the most aberrant superstitions and attempt to predict it through the most improbable means. This can be seen in practices such as divination, consulting the future through various objects. Here is a list of the most common ones:

ACUTOMANCY   Divination by means of pointed
                              objects such as pins or needles.

AEROMACY	By the movement of the winds and shapes of the clouds.
ABACOMANCY	By means of the abacus.
ACTINOMACY	Through the stars.
ALECTROMANCY	By means of a rooster.
ALEUROMANCY	Through flour.
ALOMANCY	For salt.
AMNIOMACY	Through the placenta and amniotic fluid.
ANTHROPOMANCY	Through the human entrails.
APATOMANCY	Because of the things one encounters along the way.
ARITHMOMACY	By means of the numbers associated with the letters that made up a name in some alphabets.
ARMOMANY	By inspection of a person's back.
ARPHITOMANCY	By digestion of barley bread.
ASTRAGALOMANCY	By the dice, assigning letters to each of the numbers.
ASTROMANCY	It is the precursor of astrology, augury through prophecy.
AUSTROMACY	Variety of aeromancy that specializes in winds and not in clouds.
AXYNOMACY	By means of a woodcutter's axe.

61

BELOMANCY	By means of the arrows.
BRISOMANCY	Through dreams.
BIBLIOMANCY	Through the superstitious consultation of the Holy Bible.
BOTAROMANCY	Through plants and vegetables.
CAFEMANCY	Through coffee.
CAPNOMACY	Through the air.
CARTOMANCY	Through tarot cards.
CAROMANCY	Through hypnosis or trance.
CARTOPEDIA	Through the soles of the feet.
CATOPTROMANCY / CATAXTROMANCY	By means of magic mirrors.
CEROMANCY	Through the shapes the wax takes when it melts.
CYCLOMANCY	Through rotating objects, such as a Ferris wheel or a spinning bottle.
CLEDOMISMANCY	Through words spoken without intending to say them.
CLEDOMANCY	By means of the keys wrapped in a bill and placed inside a Bible.
CLEROMANCY	By means of cubes, bones or black and white beans.
COSQUINOMANCY	By means of a sieve, sieve or sieve.
CRYSTALLOMANCY	By means of a glass ball or other glass utensil.

CRISOMANCY	Through meats and tortillas offered in sacrifice.
CHRONOMANCY	Through onions.
CDACTILOMANCY	By means of a magic ring suspended by a thread.
DAFNOMANCY	Through the laurel.
DEMONOMACY	Through demons.
ENCROMANCY	Through ink and paper.
EMPYROMANCY	By the shapes of the fire when different materials are thrown into it.
EROMANCY	Because of the air bubbles in the water.
SPODOMANCY	By the traces left in the ashes after burning the sacrifices.
EXCIAMANCY	Through the evocation of the shadows of the dead. It differs from necromancy and psycho-mancy in that it was neither the soul nor the body of the dead that was consulted, but only its image.
SPATULOMANCY	For the bones of animals.
STERNOMANCY	Through a demon who spoke through the belly or the body of a possessed person.
STOLYSOMANCY	Through the way of dressing.

STOICHOMANCY	Opening the books of Homer or Virgil.
PHILORODOMANCY	Through the petals of the rose.
GASTROMANCY	Through the stomach, which emits sounds or words.
GEOMANCY	It is done by throwing a handful of soil on the ground.
GRAPHOMANCY	By means of handwriting (not related to graphology).
GRAMATOMANCY	Through the letters of the alphabet. Within this genre is the Ouija.
HYDROMANCY	Through water.
HIPOMANCY	Through the whinnies and mooing of some white horses.
HIPOMANCY	Through the entrails of the fish.
KEPHALOMANCY	By means of the head of an ass, which was later replaced by the head of a goat.
LAMPADOMANCY	With lamps, torches and candles.
LIBANOMANCY	Through the smoke of incense.
LIGNOMANCY	Through the sparks that jump from the wick of a lamp.
LITOMANCY	Through the clash of stones.
LECANOMANCY	By means of precious stones and gold and silver leaf.
MARGARITOMANCY	By means of pearls.

MENOMANCY	Through the woman's menstruation, depending on the days on which she gets her period.
MIOMANCY	By means of rats or mice, through their squeaking or their voracity.
NECROMANCY	By evoking the dead and inspecting the corpses.
OCULOMANCY	By means of eye movement mode.
OENOMANCY	Through the color and flavor of the wine.
OFIOMANCY	By means of the movements made by the snake.
OLIOMANCY	Through the howling of dogs.
OMOMANCY	Through ram swords.
ONYCHOMANCY	By means of the glimpses given by the painted nails.
ONEIROMANCY	Through dreams.
ONOTOMANCY	Through the names of the people.
ORNITHOMANCY	By the flight or cry of the birds.
OVOMANCY	Through eggs, by reading their shells and inside them.
OSTRACOMANCY	Through oyster shells.
PARTENOMANCY	The art of guessing whether a woman is a virgin or not.
PALOMANCY	By means of prepared sticks or rods.

PEGROMANCY	By means of the springs, throwing a certain number of stones or crystals.
PETCHIMANCY	By means of brushes that remove dust on clothes.
PYROMANCY	Through fire.
PSYCOMANCY	Through the spirits.
CHIROMANCY	For the shapes and lines of the ma-nos.
RABDOMANCY	By means of sticks.
RASODOMANCY	Through poems, as in the case of Nostradamus.
SAUROMANCY	Through lizards.
SICOMANCY	With the leaves of fig trees.
SIDROMANCY thrown to the wind.	By the flashes of burnt straw
TOBACOMANCY	By tobacco or cigarette ash.
TASSEOMANCY	By means of tea leaves.
THEOMANCY	Through the name of God.
TIROMANCY	Through the worm cheese.
VITREOMANCY	With sand.

As we see from this long list of divination practices, knowing the future has been one of mankind's obsessions throughout all eras, which has enslaved him in an unsuspected way to the cunning of the evil one.

He has a special power to influence history, events, and the future of those who commit the sin of resorting to these divinatory arts. Therefore, the more one believes in and seeks divination, the more predictions come true because Satan has greater power to intervene in the lives of those who transgress God's law. In other words, a person who has never sought divination, not even through horoscopes, could be said to be the master of their own destiny, while a person who has sought divination, even just once, to know their future, has handed over to the forces of evil great power to disrupt and interfere in their future and that of future generations.

Angel magic

Angel magic is another form of witchcraft that disguises itself under the name of white magic. It attempts to establish contact with angels, even seeking to control them in order to make them do the bidding of the practitioner. In this type of magic, the concept of angels and demons, or good and evil angels, is not considered. Instead, angels are simply classified as useful or useless for achieving the desired goals. Therefore, rituals in angel magic include formulas to supposedly summon angels of God as well as fallen angels, with the intention of controlling them and obtaining a benefit depending on the morality of the invoked angel and the desired outcome, whether it is for healing or causing harm. This type of witchcraft combines not only the names of angels and demons but also those of constellations and other elements associated with witchcraft.

It is evident that good angels, knowing that God strictly prohibits all forms of superstitious magic and witchcraft, cannot cater to the whims of those who resort to these means, especially when they are outside the doctrine contained in the Holy Scripture. Therefore, those invocations of supposed good angels will actually be attended to solely and exclusively by demons. One should refrain from invoking names of angels that are not found in the Holy Scripture, as there is a risk of actually invoking a demon, as often

67

practiced in the New Age movement, where their angelology is based on pagan traditions and superstitions.

The only archangels mentioned by name in the Holy Scripture and Christian tradition are St. Michael, St. Gabriel, and St. Raphael. Therefore, we will provide a non-exhaustive list of angel names that we suspect are actually demons and that witchcraft invites people to invoke and consecrate themselves to: Kardiel, Reyel, Omagel, Vehuiha, Yahamiah, Haiaiel, Ayel, Mumiah, Nitahel, Nanael, Vehuel, Ariel, Veuliah, Aniel, Iah-hel, Chavakiah, Menadel, Seaeiah, Rehael, Haamiah, Rochel, Poiel, Leialel, Harahell, Asaliah, Manakel, Leiazel, Yezalel, Anauel, Mehiel, Damabiah, Uma-bel, Mitzarael, Harahell, Mihael, Hahahel, Mikael, Nemamiah, Habuiha, Jeliel, Sitael, Elemiah, Lehahiah, Melahel, Caliet, Hariel, Haziel, Aladiah, Laoviah, Lelahel, Achaiah, Cahethel, Lehuiah, Lecabel, Vasahiah, Leratel, Haaiah, Nith-Haheuiah, Lauviah, Leuviah, Pahalia, and Mahasiah.

Raiki

This type of witchcraft could be called energy magic. It allegedly seeks to harmonize and balance cosmic energies with the vital, spiritual, and physical energies of the human being. One of its methods is hands-on healing, which was the way God granted His apostles and disciples the ability to perform miracles. Many people practice this type of magic without knowing what they are doing, deceived by the belief that they are using divine energies. In reality, apart from the energies known in physics and chemistry, the only energies are those that originate from goodness or wickedness.

It is highly unlikely that God would allow His own energies to be used through a method outside of the Christian tradition. Hands-on healing in Reiki is dangerous due to the prayers and esoteric elements used, such as ritualized incense, perfumes, and essences, and the power to perform healings in a science transmitted through merely acquired knowledge rather than a divine gift received through fidelity to God.

I have had to attend to people who, due to practicing Reiki, have absorbed spiritual contamination from the people they attend to, which eventually leads to physical illnesses. They have required prayers of liberation and have lost God's protection.

CARE AND TREATMENT AGAINST WHITE MAGIC

This section will be found in all the following chapters, as we will outline the procedures and prayers that need to be done to counteract the effects of the analyzed magic. Since in this current chapter, we are discussing magic that supposedly doesn't cause harm to anyone except the practitioner or those who seek it, the only procedure here is to renounce witchcraft by stripping Satan of such power.

This renunciation should be done for at least nine days or until a change in the spiritual situation affecting the children or the person who sought the help of witches and diviners is noticed. It should be accompanied by attending Holy Mass and reciting the Holy Rosary daily.

Prayer of Renunciation against Witchcraft

In the name of Our Lord Jesus Christ, I renounce Satan, all witchcraft or sorcery, spiritualism or divination that I have practiced or commanded to be done.

By the power of the Blood of Christ and His glorious Cross, I take back from Satan all authority, pact, consecration, or any kind of right that because of these sins he may have over my mind, my heart, my body, my soul, my spirit, my family, my finances, or any other power he may have through the sins of my ancestors, if they practiced or resorted to the arts of darkness.

Lastly, I decree that all this authority that I am taking back from Satan today, in the name of Jesus Christ, be broken, annihilated, and destroyed in the name of Almighty God the Father, in the name of God the Son, the Redeemer of the world, in the name of God the Holy Spirit, the Defender, and by the power of binding and loosing that the Holy Catholic Church possesses, through the intercession of the most glorious ever Virgin Mary, and by the ministry of the Holy Archangels St. Michael, St. Gabriel, and St. Raphael. Amen.

Chapter IV

Green Magic

Many who categorize magic by colors claim that green magic involves the use of herbs to obtain esoteric and spiritual benefits. In addition to these uses, they are also attributed powers over prosperity and the economy of individuals. Therefore, within green magic, I want to include everything related to economic prosperity, including the practice of folk healing with its wide range of healing potions extracted from herbs and substances.

Varieties of Green Magic

Before delving into this aspect of green magic, it is important to mention that aromatherapy is also part of this type of magic. Aromatherapy seeks healing through the use of incense and essences derived from plants to harmonize affected energies.

Likewise, universal magic falls within the realm of green magic. It involves the use of the universal law of attraction to manifest desired effects. While its method is primarily mental, it differs from mere mental control by combining physical elements that carry greater power in manifesting one's desires.

Alchemy is another aspect of green magic, which seeks to transform low-value minerals such as lead or iron into high- value minerals like gold or platinum.

Out of all these aspects of green magic, we will focus on the aspects related to economy and prosperity. As for health- related aspects, it is worth noting the perspective of medical professionals on homeopathy, stating that its procedures are not scientifically proven, and if the healing effects attributed to plants were real, pharmaceutical companies would have extracted that healing power and incorporated it into conventional medicine. Therefore, if folk healing and homeopathy do provide healing, it is not due to scientific knowledge but rather the influence of some spiritual entity drawn to the superstitious means associated with such practices.

Let us now delve into this facet of green magic, which could also be called magic of luck. Its goal is to attract wealth, or in its negative form, to bring ruin upon a person. Practitioners also claim to possess the ability to predict lottery numbers, chance games, and anything related to gambling, which falls under the domain of numerology.

I want to make my readers aware that if sorcerers had the ability to accurately predict lottery numbers, they would have amassed great wealth and would not have to rely on deceiving the unsuspecting who pay them to predict such falsehoods. Considering that both gambling and divination are explicitly condemned by God in His Word, it is clear that no child of God can engage in such practices without committing a serious offense against their conscience.

Ritualized Banknotes

As an example of this type of magic, I would like to cite what we have noticed, that in many Catholics, who have been asking for a liberation from the economy, their decline in finances is closely linked to having in their possession of bills that have previously been knotted. In the case of the one-dollar bill, it is folded in such a way that only the Masonic pyramid with the eye of Satan, which is printed on the back of the bill with the inscription "Novus ordo seclorum," meaning "new order of the ages," is visible. This is understood to mean that societies will no longer be God- centered but will be under the power of diabolical anarchy. Some people have even taken banknotes to be ritualized by a sorcerer in the hope of attaining prosperity.

I remember on one occasion I was given one of these banknotes to burn, and it took me half a liter of alcohol, an hour of prayers, and almost failed to destroy it. It should have naturally succumbed to the power of the flames in less than five minutes.

Care and Treatment

If any of our readers have made the mistake of having any of these banknotes or ritualizing them, they should proceed as follows:

- They should recite the prayer of renunciation to witchcraft as described at the end of the previous chapter.
- Proceed to burn the banknote as described at the end of the first chapter, where prayers were mentioned to be recited when getting rid of encountered witchcraft.

ECONOMIC RUIN

Our Lord Jesus Christ said that we cannot serve both God and money (Matthew 6:24), implicitly declaring that money has an antagonistic nature in relation to God, that is to say, it is not one of the elements that leads easily to the Kingdom of Heaven. In fact, Jesus said that it is easier for a camel to go through the eye of a needle than for a person dedicated to the pursuit of wealth to enter the kingdom of God (Mark 10:25). Therefore, it can be said that money belongs more to the prince of this world than to our God. We cannot deny that the devil has power over the riches of this world. Let us remember that he promised all the kingdoms to Jesus if He would bow down and worship him (Matthew 4:8-9). From this, we can deduce that if our economic possessions lack God's blessing, Satan can easily devastate them, as happened in the case of Job when God withdrew His blessing.

I want us to reflect on the words that the tempter directs to God in Job 1:9-11: "Does Job fear God for nothing? Have you not put a hedge around him and his household and everything he has? You have blessed the work of his hands, so that his flocks and herds are spread throughout the land. But now stretch out your hand and strike everything he has, and he will surely curse you to your face."

This statement by Satan enlightens us, particularly about the protective power that comes from God's blessing on our economic possessions. The tempter himself acknowledges that he cannot touch Job's possessions because the spiritual hedge of God's blessing keeps him immune against all his attacks.

Secondly, these words shed light on the fact that all children of God should enjoy the same divine hedge of protection over their finances. Therefore, if someone complains of economic difficulties, it can be attributed to either not living as a true child of God, and thus God has not protected their possessions, or, in the case of a righteous and upright person who fears God and shuns evil, as the Bible describes Job, it could be a possibility that they are being tested in their faithfulness to see if their love for money is not greater than their love for God. For according to the words of the devil, that was the essence of the test - to see if Job would not curse God for taking away everything He had given him.

In my experience as a missionary over the years, after having met thousands of Catholics, is that very few Catholics are aware that we also need to worship God with our money. As I often say, they are accustomed to loving and serving God only from the belly button up, as the faith professed by 95% of Catholics does not include their wallet.

This lack of awareness in the economic worship, which unfortunately our separated brethren do possess, is what makes Catholics so vulnerable to hexes of economic ruin.

I want to mention a case of a practicing Catholic family who had a business that was generating a monthly income of 120 million pesos. However, due to envy and some curses of ruin that were cast upon them, they had fallen into a desperate state where they could no longer afford to even put gas in their cars. They had lost a hotel and a property valued at 1 billion pesos, which was already seized by the bank. In this state of urgency, they turned to me for help.

As I usually do in such cases, I taught them about the need to sanctify their finances through tithing in order to attain the protective hedge that holy Job had. My words certainly caused discomfort, as they always do when I speak to people who hold money closer to their hearts than God. They argued that when they were doing well, they used to donate 3 million pesos a year to a poor parish. I replied that 3 million pesos a year was not ten percent of 120 million pesos per month, which caused even more unease. In fact, the priest who referred the case to me told me that these people were very upset with me, because I had told them that if they didn't tithe with me, I wouldn't pray for their deliverance.

I replied to my priest friend that I had already performed the deliverance prayer in their presence, and I had broken all the curses, envy, and evil spells. However, I had to talk to them about tithing so that the prayers would have maximum efficacy and they wouldn't make the mistake of leaving their finances vulnerable to Satan's plunder again. I never told them they had to tithe with me. In fact, I mentioned that they should tithe with the priest they trusted the most because they needed that priestly blessing to restore the divine hedge of protection. However, their hearts were hardened by the love of money, and they felt pain in giving to God. Because of that, God would never bless their businesses. And even though it hurt, I had to warn them so that they wouldn't later say that my prayers were useless and they were still stuck in ruin.

My priest friend told me not to talk to Catholics about money if I didn't want to make enemies who would slander me, just like those good Catholics were doing. I replied that I wouldn't stop preaching the truth out of fear of men. I knew that sanctifying finances through tithes, offerings, and first fruits was the only way to escape economic ruin induced by witchcraft. I wouldn't stop preaching the truth, even if they turned against me and attacked me.

With all of the above, we take for granted that the Holy Scriptures affirm that Satan can have power over the finances of the children of God if the Lord Himself allows it. Now, let us proceed to describe some symptoms that, in practice, may lead us to suspect that we are being affected by one of these hexes:

Symptoms of the hex of economic ruin

- *Difficulty in finding employment* or in persevering in the ones obtained. This means that, assuming the person affected is competent and performs their work well compared to their colleagues, they notice a constant struggle in their life to secure new jobs or to maintain employment for more than eight days.

- *Physical disappearance* of money or money not yielding as it should. Once the possibilities of someone stealing the money by the security methods used, the person realizes that the money physically disappears, either partially or entirely, or that despite having money in their pocket, they are unsure of how it was spent.

  I encountered a case where, despite having a hidden safe in a location known only to one person, the money disappeared entirely or partially. This phenomenon did not cease until I performed an exorcism on the safe and anointed it with exorcised oil.

  I was also told by a gentleman that the hex of economic ruin placed upon him was of such a nature, it was enough for him to put some money in his pocket for it to slip out, even without moving or sitting down, as if an invisible hand would take it out and throw it to the ground. His own wife confirmed witnessing this phenomenon on numerous occasions, she would notice that her husband could be calmly conversing with someone or standing in line at the bank without moving, and she would see the money mysteriously slipping out of his pocket and falling to the ground without his awareness. She would then alert him to the fact that his money was falling. He himself confessed that on several occasions, honest people would stop him on the street to tell him that he had just dropped some money. There was no doubt in his mind that this was a supernatural phenomenon, as he rarely managed to come home with the money he earned. Interestingly, this hex would erase his awareness of losing the money and mysteriously create the sensation that he had spent it on something.

I present these examples here, even though some may consider them trivial because I know that many people reading them will gain clarity about events that were previously inexplicable to them. As I told this family, it is amusing to see how many individuals have experiences with these spiritual phenomena but keep them silent out of fear of being considered crazy. However, when I give a lecture or speak about these matters, everyone says, "That happened to me too" or "A relative told me similar things," and they only open up when they find someone else who believes in these phenomena, someone as "crazy" as they are.

Well, regardless of whether they think I'm crazy, let's continue moving forward, shedding light and clarity for those who are willing to believe and want to protect themselves against so much existing wickedness.

- *Appliance breakdowns.* It is normal for an electrical appliance to occasionally break down, but when under the influence of a curse of economic ruin, household appliances start to systematically malfunction or burn out one after another, without any fluctuations in electrical voltage in the area, eventually leaving the household with virtually no functioning appliances.

I met a young man in Argentina who invited me to his house for a prayer of liberation. He explained to me that at that moment, all his appliances were broken, from the blender, air conditioner, microwave, DVD player, to his car, and the only thing still working was a small cassette player that had been given to him, but he knew that it would also become damaged once it reached the fifteen- day mark. At first, he thought the cause was an electrical failure, but after checking the entire electrical installation, he concluded that everything was in order. Not satisfied with this, he investigated with all his neighbors to see if they were experiencing the same issues, in case there was a high voltage from the power plant causing damage to everyone's appliances at the same frequency as his. Surprised to find that none of his neighbors had reported any problems with the electrical current, he decided to seek my help because it was evident that if there were no natural causes, everything was due to a supernatural cause. When we performed the prayer of liberation, we confirmed that indeed an ex-girlfriend had placed an economic binding spell on him, causing him to suffer from alarming financial hardship and preventing him from marrying his current wife. I like to cite this example to enlighten my listeners, and in this case, my readers, on how we should first seek logical and natural causes for our problems before alarming ourselves by thinking that we are the target of a hex or economic binding.

Therefore, the person who identifies one of these elements should not necessarily worry, as it is necessary to rule out all logical possibilities before considering oneself a victim of a hex of economic ruin. But if the person finds that there are no coherent reasons to explain the origin of the phenomena they are experiencing and realizes that at least one of these three elements cannot be clarified through equanimity reasoning, then it is time to put forth their effort and focus on the solutions we are going to propose:

Care and treatment

Let's propose three pillars that form the foundation of blessed and protected finances by our God. These three elements, which we will further develop, are: first, fortifying the economy through first fruits, tithes, and offerings.

Secondly, gratitude, and thirdly, breaking generational curses of ruin.

Shield the Economy

To prevent Satan from continuing to feast on our material possessions, we must attain a blessing as great as the one Job had over his possessions, which made the devil say that he could not touch them until God lifted that blessing. This blessing of economic fortification is achieved through proper economic worship to God, which involves recognizing in a tangible way that everything we have comes exclusively from our Father God.

If we analyze the Scriptures, we will find that God elaborates a detailed economic liturgy based primarily on first fruits, tithes, and offerings. Before explaining each of these elements of the financial liturgy contained in the Scriptures, I want to make it clear that if Christ said, "Give to Caesar what is Caesar's and to God what is God's" in Mark 12:17, and no Catholic complains about giving taxes to the government, such as the VAT on each of our purchases, why do we become scandalized when a preacher tells us that we should give ten percent to God?

If we truly understood that everything we have, starting with life, health, intellectual capacity, work, businesses, clients –

absolutely everything – comes from God, it would seem only right to pay the divine tax first, without neglecting the human tax afterwards.

With this introduction and considering that Christ did not come to abolish the Old Testament but to fulfill it, let us now explain the mechanics of the financial worship prescribed by God.

The first element commanded by God is that of first fruits, which consisted of consecrating to God the first fruits of our enterprises and projects. By offering these initial material gifts to the Lord, we attract His blessing upon the rest of our projects or businesses.

For example, in the case of the Jews, God asked them in Leviticus 23:10, "When you enter the land I am giving you and you reap its harvest, bring to the priest a sheaf of the first grain you harvest." In Numbers 15:21, God asks for the separation of the first fruits from the ground grain, and in Deuteronomy 26:2, He asks for the presentation of the first fruits from all the products of the soil.

The amount of the first fruits is relatively small compared to the total harvest. This is because not all the fruit of the planting had been harvested yet, from which they would later have to give a tithe. The objective was simply to embrace or surround the entire harvest with two sublime acts of faith: first fruits and tithes. This way, all the work of man would be enveloped in acts of faith, hope, and love for God, attracting His protection, blessing, and prosperity.

In the case of Jews who relied on livestock, the first fruits involved sacrificing the firstborn of each animal before God. For example, in Numbers 18:17, it is required to sacrifice every firstborn cow, sheep, or goat. The first fruits are so significant in God's perspective that He even claims the firstborns from human wombs. However, in Exodus 13:13 and 34:20, there is the provision that the firstborns of humans must be redeemed with a lamb. The firstborn of a donkey, which was the ordinary means of transportation for the people of God, could also be redeemed with a lamb or left unredeemed. We should not forget the sentence contained at the end of the latter verse, which says, "And no one shall appear before me empty- handed."

I recall a woman who invited me to perform a deliverance for her company, which had gone from great prosperity to almost bankruptcy. She couldn't understand why God had stopped blessing her and allowed envy, curses, and malevolent spells to almost destroy her business. Furthermore, she told me that she had officially appointed the Sacred Heart of Jesus as the company's manager and took me to the manager's office, where the painting of the Sacred Heart was enthroned. However, her tone of fervor and kindness abruptly changed when I asked her what salary she had set for that manager. She told me there was no salary. I explained to her that if she wanted God to be a partner in her business and invest all His omnipotence to ensure its prosperity, He had already stipulated in the Holy Scriptures that His managerial salary was set at 10% of the net profits. Obviously, such a statement did not sit well with the pious woman, and I believe that was where our friendship ended, but her indignation didn't prevent me from performing the necessary prayers, even though I knew that, like the Sacred Heart, I was also not going to receive very good remuneration for my services. So I proceeded to perform all the necessary rituals, even though I knew that due to her hardened heart, my time and prayers would not be very effective. And I want to reiterate that I never said that she had to give those tithes to me, but rather to the priest in whom she had the most trust, so that he could bless her finances in the name of God. And since we touched on tithes with this example, let's clarify a bit the reason and nature of tithes.

When we talk about tithing, we are not referring to one day's salary per year, as the Catholic Church has had to ask due to the hardness of its followers' hearts, but rather we are referring to one-tenth of all net income of any kind that one possesses.

81

For example, in Leviticus 27:30, the Lord decrees that one must tithe from every product of the land, both from seeds and fruit trees, and affirms that it is a sacred thing of Yahweh. Similarly, in Leviticus 27:32, it is decreed that the people must tithe from all livestock, giving every tenth head that passes under the shepherd's staff. The Letter to the Hebrews 7:2 also tells us that Abraham tithed to the high priest Melchizedek one-tenth of everything he had gained in his military campaign.

Therefore it is a mistake to think that the commandment of Church requires tithing only once a year, but should rather be understood as asking, at a minimum, to tithe the at least once a year, just as he similarly commands that we all confess at least once a year, which does not prevent that we confess as many times as the state of our hearts consciences require it.

Furthermore, using texts like Deuteronomy 14:22, which states that you should set aside the tithe each year, is illogical and would be an invalid excuse for our time. That mandate was for an agricultural people who only harvested once a year, so it couldn't demand a monthly tithe from them.

But since our current economic system provides monthly income and each of those monthly earnings should be recognized as a blessing from God, we should give acknowledgment of it through monthly tithing. Just as we declare occasional earnings to the government and pay taxes for it, we should also tithe to God for the same reason. The effect of tithing is to ensure that God's blessing is constant month after month, while the first fruits would be a way to consecrate the beginning of a project, the fruits of which are unknown, so that God can make those fruits abundant.

Therefore, it is sad to see that there are many people who prefer to have 100% of nothing because sooner or later they will lose God's blessing by stealing what belongs to Him. They do not choose to have 90% of everything, which ensures the constancy of God's provision through tithing. And that withholding tithes constitutes a sin of theft is evident in the book of Malachi 3:8-9: "Will a man rob God? Yet you have robbed me! But you say, 'In what way have we robbed you?' In tithes and in the reserved offering. You are cursed with a curse, for you have robbed me, even this whole nation." In Deuteronomy 12:17, it says, "You may not eat within your gates the tithe of your grain or your new wine or your oil, nor the firstborn of your herds or your flocks, nor any of your offerings which you vow, nor you're freewill offerings or the heave offering of your hand." And in Jeremiah 2:3, "Whoever devours it will be held guilty; disaster will come upon him."

It is incredible to consider the large number of those who call themselves practicing Catholics, but in reality, trample upon these mandates and then hypocritically complain that God has turned His back on their businesses.

A great number of children of the Catholic Church are watching television, talking on the latest generation cell phones, paying for internet, going to the gym, and spending money on cosmetic surgeries, all while robbing God of tithes. It is true that not everyone does it with full awareness, as in this matter, and in almost all the topics we have discussed in this book, there has been a lack of instruction from the pastors of the Catholic Church. They fear what others will say and prefer to see their flock ravaged by wolves rather than being accused of trying to exploit their faithful, leaving them vulnerable to the evils of economic ruin caused by witchcraft.

To those priests who read my book, I say from my experience that even if we don't speak or ask for money, the Judases who have infiltrated our Church will still complain that the wealth of Rome does not go to the poor. But I say the same as St. John, that those Catholics do not care about the poor, but rather, what they want is to continue stealing the tithes of the Lord without their conscience accusing them. What I have noticed is that faithful individuals with good hearts can identify when a priest is dedicating themselves and exhausting themselves for the work of the Lord, and they have no qualms about giving to God. The more we preach about tithing, the more they will be blessed, and the more generously they will give to the Lord.

I dare to use as an example the Protestant sects, which are mostly composed of dissident Catholics. As long as no one preached to them about tithing, they never gave it. However, once they joined a Protestant Church where they were made aware of the sacred duty of tithing, they not only limited themselves to giving a tenth to their pastors, but they gave abundantly in the realm of offerings, which we will discuss later.

But before we move on to offerings, I want to analyze some texts that Protestant pastors never preach on. In these texts, God designates His priests as the exclusive delegates to collect tithes. Nowhere in the Holy Scriptures does it say that a layperson can receive tithes on behalf of the Lord. At most, they could receive an offering based on what Galatians 6:6 says, that the disciple should share all good things with the one who instructs them in the word.

A young lawyer came to me who wanted to start working independently, fighting for justice for so many elderly people whose pensions the government refused to pay. She was faced with the dilemma of not wanting to charge them as much upfront as her colleagues in the profession did, as many of the elderly were practically destitute. She only wanted to charge them a modest sum of 250,000.00 Colombian Pesos, the necessary amount to start the whole process, unlike her colleagues who asked for over a million. This woman of faith had made a covenant with God to tithe to the Church for every successful case. Since she didn't have her first client yet, she decided to give the first fruits of those 250,000 Colombian pesos she planned to charge to the first client that appeared. She decided to give 25,000 Colombian Pesos as the first fruits, which would be like tithing from that initial fee of 250,000 Colombian pesos, asking for the blessing for the Lord to send her many cases to defend and win, so she could collect her percentage and tithe from it.

It didn't take long to see the fruits of this act of faith, as she managed to secure 33 cases to handle. So when she won the first ones, she immediately went to the priest to receive the blessing for the next litigation, and the blessings were so great that at the time of writing these words, she had already won 32 out of the 33 cases she had obtained, in a timeframe that her colleagues in the profession considered a record in terms of how quickly they were resolved.

I want to encourage my fellow priests not to deprive their flock of the blessings that God has reserved for them if they fulfill their tithes, as it says in Malachi 3:10: "Bring the full tithe into the storehouse, that there may be food in my house. And thereby put me to the test, says the Lord of hosts, if I will not open the windows of heaven for you and pour down for you a blessing until there is no more need. I will rebuke the devourer for you, so that it will not destroy the fruits of your soil, and your vine in the field shall not fail to bear fruit, says the Yavhé Sebaot."

Note that in this text, the liberating power of tithing is clearly seen, which is why I decided to elaborate on it. Here it is declared that tithing has the power to rebuke the devourer, who is Satan, and thus make us immune to all the economic binding that can lead to the destruction of our assets and the barrenness of our businesses and projects.

Having discussed the significance of first fruits and tithing in the financial liturgy, which are ordained to ensure constancy and blessings that come from God, let us now analyze what offerings are. They could be called the sowing, because just as sowing one grain of rice yields a hundred, when a faithful Catholic ventures to sow through offerings, the constant fruit that is assured by first fruits and tithing will increase both in quantity and yield.

Offerings in the Scriptures were given for various reasons. For example, to consecrate an altar (Numbers 7:11), as atonement for a sin committed (Leviticus 9:7), for the construction of a temple (Exodus 35:21), to fulfill a vow (Numbers 15:3), and as an act of thanksgiving (2 Corinthians 9:12).

To emphasize the gravity and seriousness with which God regards offerings, especially when they come from a vow or promise on our part, I want to begin by analyzing the text in the Acts of the Apostles 5:1 and following, where Ananias and Sapphira had promised to give all the money from the sale of a property.

By common agreement, both spouses decided to keep part of what they had promised to give, which caused St. Peter, the first pope, to decree in the name of God their death, since they had defrauded the Lord himself and it is not that the first Christians have killed them for having failed to comply with the offering they promised, but Ananias fell dead first when he was discovered by St. Peter and to be seen that it was not a coincidence, but a prophecy that decreed the death of these thieves, when they came to bury her husband Sapphira fell dead.

As can be seen, the intention with which the offerings are made is not a matter of keeping up appearances, but it could be said that it is a matter of life or death. Lest I be misunderstood, what I mean is that, although it will not always deprive us of bodily life, what I am affirming is that with this example Sacred Scripture shows us that it does put eternal life at risk.

One of the words that St. Peter pronounced in the sentence against Ananias and Sapphira, and that all modern Catholics should keep in mind, is the one contained in verse 4: "Did you not have him for yourself without selling him, and when he was sold, was the price not at your disposal? Why did you determine in your heart to do this? You have not lied to men but to God". These words of our first pope shed light on the mentality that we should all have about the disposition of our economic goods, which have always belonged to us because God gave them to us, and if we want to make God a participant of those economic goods as a reasonable worship, we must do so knowing that it is to God Himself that we give or withhold them, and not to men, even though it is they who must receive them from God.

Therefore we must keep in mind that what we give must be in accordance with the dignity of the one whom we intend to worship with our economy, and that we must avoid with all our heart making our offerings just to keep up appearances before men. We see that the economic worship that God established in his people is too detailed and complete, to despise or ignore it as we currently do. The saddest thing is that many limit themselves to giving the minimum at the moment of the offerings in the Holy Mass and that is why we Catholics are taken by the Protestant pastors as an example of what should not be done, for one of them said: "Do not be like the Catholics who think that God is a beggar, who is content with a few coins, for He is the owner and lord of heaven and earth and should be given an economic worship reasonable to His dignity".

Certainly they are hurtful words, but I use them because sadly they are not without truth, because I usually reason with my Catholics telling them: "If you were reduced to misery and your wife and children were starving, you approach a relative who is well off, you ask him to help you and that wealthy relative tells you that of course, you can count on him and takes out of his pocket a coin of 500 or a bill of 1000 Colombian pesos, with which you know that in our country not even a soda can be bought, would you not feel indignant, for the insult that such a miserable amount represents for your needs. Well, how much more will your God feel indignant to see that after having benefited you with all that you have, you condense all your gratitude in your usual paltry offerings".

I know that many shield themselves by saying that they do not trust the priests, because they do not know what they are going to spend the money of the tithes and offerings on, but to that I usually answer that although I accept that there are certainly some priests who are shameless in the use and abuse of God's patrimony, not all are the same and we have to keep in mind two things: first, that God imposed this obligation of tithing and offering, and although the offering could be given to the poor, the tithe is exclusive to the priest and therefore there will be the duty to look for a pious priest with whom to fulfill the obligation. Secondly, in the case that necessity presses and we find it necessary to deposit our tithe with an unworthy priest, we must keep in mind that the faithful will only be asked to account for whether he gave or did not give, whether he fulfilled or did not fulfill his sacred duty of tithing; On the other hand, he will not be asked to account for what the priest does with those tithes, since God Himself will demand an exquisite account of what he did with that sacred money, as is shown by many testimonies of mystics who have seen priests burn in hell, even for having received stipends without the intention of celebrating those masses. How much more when they receive the tithe from God to be administered and distributed between their worthy sustenance and the sustenance of the poor, orphans and widows.

To end this part of this chapter, I want to cite two examples that touched my heart regarding tithes and offerings.

The first one is of a gentleman who came to me suffering from an economic binding caused because a person to whom he had lent money had conjured a spell of ruin to finish with him, so that he would not have to repay what he owed him; this spell had so tied up his economy that other businesses he had were totally blocked, so that he was at risk of losing a lot of money that he had lent to other people.

As always I catechized him about the liberating power of tithing and asked him to make a covenant with God by offering him ten percent of each money that the Lord was returning to him, which he had already given up for lost. Obviously I told him that he could tithe with any priest he trusted, but I warned him to demand that he bless his economy, for it was not enough to reach the fence of divine blessing for the priest to simply thank him for the tithe by putting it in his pocket, but he had to use his priestly power to attract God's blessing on the tither's economy.

He began to do it this way and it was pleasant to find him some time later happy, because thanks to his faithfulness in tithing, he had managed to recover almost all the money he had lent, he was waiting to receive the little that was left pending, something that also filled me with gratitude towards God, to see that this seed had been sown in fertile soil that gave one hundred percent in its harvest.

The other example about the offerings is very similar to that of the widow in the Gospel who threw in her little coins, of what she had to live on, but who was immediately detected by the paternal gaze of God.

A woman came to me to testify that when she heard me preach about the liberating power of offerings, she only had 2,000 Colombian pesos in her pocket for the bus fare and decided to make the sacrifice of going on foot to make this humble offering to her Lord.

God's response was not long in coming, as she testified that the day after she made this act of faith, hope and love for God and even sacrifice, she was given back 200,000 Colombian pesos that she had lent a long time ago and that she had thought she had lost.

I would have many other examples to share of people who got jobs the moment they promised to tithe with God, after months of being unemployed, and of multitudes of people who have even achieved miracles of healing and deliverance for having opted for generosity in their offerings. The reason for this is because there has never been in history any man or woman who can say that he or she has beaten God in generosity.

Gratitude

Having seen the three elements that shield our economy, first fruits, tithes and offerings, let us move on to another factor that is intimately linked to the abundance or famine in which many people may be living, and that is gratitude.

Many Catholics, like the nine lepers who were healed (Luke 17:17), forget to give thanks for the goods received from the hand of God, food, health, work, prosperity; which is the cause of Jesus' indignation with which he said: "Where are the other nine who were also healed?!"

Therefore, we strongly recommend to our readers that they do not fail to send to celebrate frequently holy masses of thanksgiving for all the favors received from our Heavenly Father, particularly in special moments such as the birth of a child, getting a job, opening a business, buying a house, a vehicle, etc.; taking advantage of this occasion to give a tithe or offering that represents in the eyes of God the value we give to the gift received.

The reason for this dates from before, because Moses already commanded that whoever received a favor from God should present himself at the altar of God with an offering or a sacrifice, as Jesus invites the lepers he heals, to present themselves before the priest and pay the stipulated offering for the miracle received.

The importance of gratitude lies in the fact that no one likes to benefit the ungrateful who do not know how to value what they receive. For example, I knew the case of a woman who had been asking the Lord for the grace to be able to conceive a child, even though she was missing an ovary and the doctors said it was impossible in those conditions. In a prayer group, the woman felt a prick in her remaining ovary and she received within herself the motion that this was the miracle she was asking for. Unfortunately, the woman got carried away with the doctors' diagnosis of her inability to conceive and began to tell herself that it was it is all in the mind and not a reality. In the face of such ingratitude, God withdrew His grace and the supernaturally conceived baby was lost in a miscarriage.

When she received the medical result of the bleeding as spontaneous loss of a baby, she repented and committed to God to never ever doubt His mercy.

As the Lord is rich in mercy, he performed the miracle again and now her daughter is seventeen years old. Here we can see the importance of being grateful for what we receive from God and not despise miracles as if they were trinkets, but we must appreciate them in all their splendor as divine gifts.

Breaking intergenerational curses of ruin

About the power that the sins of our ancestors have, we will already discuss in the chapter on other spiritual threats the intergenerational force of sin. Here we will say that the sins committed by our ancestors of greed, ambition, theft or swindling, together with the curses they have uttered or received, can affect our economy today, so we must not fail to make prayers of intergenerational breaking of sin, as we will see below to reduce the influence we may have on our finances.

Prayer for protection and breaking of financial ruin

Before citing the prayer of breaking, I would like to point out that what is important is not the number of prayers, but the intensity with which they are prayed. Remember that the intensity of faith in Christ must be greater than that which the sorcerer has in Satan.

We also recommend that a prayer be made over the money received, since it has been proven that material things can acquire a certain spiritual contamination, depending on the sinful purpose for which they have been used. Also, the money that has been used by other holders, for example, to commit sins such as homicide, to pay for prostitution, pornography, extortion, bribes, etc., acquire a curse from God that can make the situation even more difficult for the people affected by a hex of economic ruin.

To exemplify the way sin can contaminate money, I want to relate what happened to me with a young man in Argentina, who, to show me his gratitude, brought me an offering. When I received these bills I felt that they burned in my hand and I asked the young man if they had been given to him or where he had gotten them from, because I noticed that they were quite contaminated. The young man told me that they had come directly from the bank, but he reddened with embarrassment when he saw that I assured him that there was something wrong with these bills and that we had to find the cause. In the end he had to confess that he had actually taken the money out of his parents' business without authorization. Upon learning this I returned the offering to him, asked him to take it to his father and notify him of his decision to give it to me and that if his father approved I would receive it later, but if not, return it to him.

The poor boy humbly accepted the correction and went to his father, the next day he returned happy saying that his father had approved the donation, immediately after, he handed it back to me and in my hands it did not cause any discomfort.

With this experience I gave thanks to God, because it showed me how sin could spiritually mark the objects, and that perhaps if I had introduced that offering, so contaminated in my patrimony, it would have affected it, binding it in some way.

I know that not all people have this spiritual sensitivity to detect this type of phenomena, but it is enough to use the sacramentals on the money that comes to our patrimony, to drive away the contamination that has not been acquired by our fault or by that of our ancestors.

I end this chapter knowing that the Pharisee will not fail to say: why do we dedicate so many pages to this subject? But so great is the havoc that economic ruin is causing in my sheep and such is the ignorance, that it is my pastoral duty to instruct them and give them the medicine that is needed, even if it is bitter.

Economic ruin breakup prayer

In the name of Our Lord Jesus Christ, by the power of His Precious Blood and His Holy Cross, I break, untie and dissolve all envy, curse or hex that has fallen on my finances because of the evil of my enemies, my own infidelities in not fulfilling the tithe for the Church or because of the sins and injustices of my ancestors that may be impeding the economic blessings that God has for me.

I wash with the Blood of Our Lord Jesus Christ all spiritual contamination that has fallen on my economic goods because of the sins that the people who gave them to me or the sins that I have committed with them have committed with them.

I invoke the Providence of God upon my patrimony, so that God's blessing may multiply it and make it yield, and I commit myself from this very moment to set aside 10% of all my income to give it to the Church.

Finally, I appoint the Blessed Virgin Mary as administrator of all my belongings so that with them I may obtain the eternal wealth of the Kingdom of her Son. Amen.

Chapter V
Red magic

As we saw before, depending on the school of witchcraft, the meaning changes according to the color. In the case of red magic in the magic school of Santeria, it is called blood magic. In it, animal sacrifices are used, from which the intention is to extract the power to harm, from which it is derived that this genre belongs more properly to black magic, which we will see later.

We are going to study it according to what it means for most of the schools, where it is called love magic, and it is the one that through its arts tries to manipulate the feelings of the people causing fortuitous infatuations, by means of a spiritual violence infused in the victim, through spells and drinks, in such a way that the affected person yields to the amorous intentions and even to the indecent proposals of the one who sends to elaborate this evil spell.

Thanks to this type of magic, sexual incompatibilities, divorces or even to the excess of inducing someone to sexual debauchery can be achieved.

If someone wants to be convinced of the existence of this type of magic, it is enough to open the classified ads of any of the existing newspapers, where you will find ads in which services are openly offered to bind, bind, return loved ones, regardless of the time of separation or distance, or even if you are married to another person.

This type of magic is more common than anyone can think. In fact, I have had cases of men who have come to my days of liberation, yielding to the request of their wives, but without believing that they could be affected by this type of magic, and after starting the prayers they have been surprised to find themselves vomiting semen with clots of menstrual blood, which are the elements used to sexually bind a man to his sporadic mistresses, so that these men become obsessed in a wild way to these females, so much so that they begin to be repulsed to have relations with their own wives.

But the sad thing about this is that these arts do not stop there, but even affect the spouses themselves, who for no reason begin to feel some repudiation by the presence of her husband, and even in such a way are tied sexually, that they come to feel violated in the sexual act with her husband by the pain that this produces.

When red magic aims not only to separate the couple, but it also tries to damage or atrophy sexuality or cause diseases such as uterine cancer in the innocent wives, of breasts and even sterility so that they cannot give their husbands the fruit of their wombs, then this enters into the realm of blue magic, as we will see later on.

MARITAL DIVISION

One of the most famous elements of red magic, and the one most frequently used today, is that of marital division, which seeks to separate a couple in order to keep the husband or wife to whom they are sentimentally and sexually attached, which we will see later on.

Obviously here we will deal with the marital division caused by the evil spell and not by the natural causes of infidelity or lack of psychosentimental compatibility between the spouses. From the point of view of faith, we can find in the Holy Scriptures diabolical interventions, oriented to prevent the consummation of a marriage, as is the case of Tobit 3, 8, where it is stated that Sarah, who was to be Tobiah's wife, had a diabolical oppression of the demon

Asmodeus who had taken the lives of seven men who had tried to consummate their marriage with her.

From this text I want to draw two conclusions that should serve for reflection of the people who do not believe in the diabolic power to influence the current life of human beings: first, that here it is affirmed that this demon had power over the life of seven men, from where it follows that if God allows it, the death spells that some sorcerers make can have effectiveness and, second, that this diabolic oppression was directly linked to the fact of the marriage, for it is said that only this demon attempted against the life of men who tried to have their first relationship with Sara.

For this brutalized world, thanks to atheistic rationalism, to believe in these matters that we are dealing with is impossible, but in my daily experience and in my continuous struggle not to put obstacles to faith, I have had ample proof of the interest that the infernal forces have in putting an end to sacramental marriage.

The first thing we have to think about is the advantages that the enemy of souls gains by destroying Catholic marriages. Marriages by the Church and blessed with the gift of children, are the cellular nucleus of the Catholic Church, where in most cases is the only place where indoctrination and example of life and faith, which sometimes in the churches is not received so clearly and faithful to the Catholic, apostolic and Roman tradition, continues to be received.

Once the union of the spouses is broken, except on rare occasions, both spouses will end up falling into adultery, which originates a chain of sins that will necessarily affect the behavior and even the faith of the children.

Rare are the cases in which children of a marriage that has ended in divorce want to contract nuptials in their lives, since, according to their utopian excuse, they do not want to marry to prevent their children from suffering what they suffered with the divorce of their parents.

As can be seen, the victory that Satan achieves by dividing a marriage is manifold, especially if the children who suffer the separation of their parents are very young, the lack of the paternal or maternal figure will cause in them later on a great difficulty to embrace with love, the idea of a God as father or of the Virgin Mary as spiritual mother, depending on the paternal or maternal lack they have had, as it has already been demonstrated in the studies carried out by the Catholic Charismatic Renewal in the matter of inner healing.

The children thus affected will be easy victims for the satanic seductions hidden subliminally in cartoons and video games, as I have said so many times in my lectures on Satanism in cartoons, or in the case of young people the subliminals hidden in Latin music and rock music, as I have also demonstrated in the international congresses I have given on the subject.

As can be seen, the consequences of marital division are catastrophic and always beneficial to the forces of evil, which fight for the total eradication of the Church. That is why my reflection is aimed at opening our eyes, in order to stop, as far as possible, this cancer that the Catholic Church has and which is called divorce.

In the days of liberation that I usually do, several couples have already presented themselves to me, who confess that after having loved each other with great intensity and understood each other perfectly, unexpectedly a certain distance began to develop between them. With the passing of time, fights began to arise that had no cause proportionate to the violence with which they assaulted each other, moreover the common denominator was to be surprised by the aggressive way in which they hurt each other after the argument had already passed.

They also noticed that in their sexual relations they began to feel a certain incompatibility, which did not allow mutual satisfaction in the marital act.

In these cases there was always behind some ex-boyfriend or ex-girlfriend who had resorted to red magic to prevent the happiness of the person with whom they were sentimentally linked. We have discovered that this type of evil is usually done with a photo of the marriage that is stolen by the person who wants to send evil to be done, which delivers it to the sorcerer to be subsequently wrapped with cemetery soil mixed with dog and cat hair.

This evil spell seeks, with the cemetery earth, the death of the feelings of affection and love between the couple, and the dog and cat hairs seek to cause arguments and fights as these species of animals usually have.

Care and treatment

To dissolve this type of evil we recommend a renewal of the marriage vows, preferably in front of a priest, who should also renew his priestly blessing on the union. After this both spouses will make with great faith the following prayer of breaking the evil spells of marital division, reclaiming each other's hearts and expelling from them any other person who tries to come between them and the love they promised each other at the Altar of God.

Renewal of marriage commitment

The wife says: I N.N. renew the sacrament of matrimony before our God, and I declare that it is my desire to renew my promise to be faithful to my husband in joy and in sorrow, in sickness and in health, to love and respect him as long as we both shall live, and to let nothing separate us until our passage into eternity.

The husband: I, N.N., renew the sacrament of matrimony before our God, and I declare that it is my desire to renew my promise to be faithful to my wife in joy and in sorrow, in sickness and in health, to love and respect her for as long as we both shall live, and to let nothing separate us until our passage into eternity.

Both of us together: having thus renewed the strength of the Sacrament of Matrimony which unites us, in the name of Our Lord Jesus Christ and by virtue of the power of the Sacrament of Matrimony, we expel from us any person, spirit or demon, and we break every envy, curse or evil spell which attempts to separate what God has united. This we decree in the name of God the Father Almighty, in the name of God the Son Redeemer of the world, in the name of God the Holy Spirit Defender, and by the power of binding and loosing which Holy Mother Catholic Church has, through the intercession of the most glorious ever Virgin Mary and through the ministry of the Holy Archangels St. Michael, St. Gabriel and St. Raphael. Amen.

They will pray the prayer found at the end of this chapter, every time it is necessary until the effects of the marital division disappear.

MOORING POTIONS

Another point that we must take into account that refers to this type of magic are the bindings or ties, which are made to attract a person with whom you want to have a romantic relationship.

This type of sentimental and sexual ties can be done in different ways. One of the most common, as we have already mentioned, is when the woman wants to tie the man, so that he only has eyes for her. Most often this is done through a potion or a spell that is made with the male's semen and menstrual blood, plus some prayers and incantations.

This makes the man feel an irresistible attraction towards the woman and even though he does not stop loving his wife, he cannot stop thinking about the woman who is binding him. Obviously it is necessary to clarify that this type of evil is not equally effective in all men, because the more pious they are and the more prayer they make, the less powerfully they will be dragged after sin.

What is a common denominator is that every man will realize that he is being violented by passion, and even that he does not know himself in the attitudes and things he is capable of doing to be with the woman who has bound him.

Care and treatment

In this case it is recommended that the affected person, every day on an empty stomach, drink a small glass of exorcised water, and if you also have the salt and oil, you can combine them asking our Lord Jesus Christ to break any spell, filter, tie or tie, sentimental or sexual of which you are a victim.

This should be done until the drink is expelled by vomiting or by diarrhea, in the case of women it can also be expelled by an early menstrual period.

Remember that everything that goes beyond the use of the sacraments and sacramentals of the Church enters into the realm of superstition, and therefore the use of it will be a new source of contamination and worsening of the situation.

Prayer for breaking of Magic Potion

In the name of Our Lord Jesus Christ I renounce Satan, I renounce adultery, fornication and any kind of unbridled sex, and I reclaim my spiritual, sentimental and sexual freedom, and I acknowledge Our Lord Jesus Christ as the only Lord and master of my life, my mind, my heart and my body, and by the power of His Most Precious Blood I break and loose every binding that has been made to me with blood or impure fluids and expel them from me in the name of God the Father Almighty, in the name of God the Son Redeemer of the world, in the name of God the Holy Spirit Defender, and by the power of the Holy Mother Catholic Church to bind and loose, through the intercession of the most glorious ever Virgin Mary and through the ministry of the Holy Archangels St. Michael, St. Gabriel and St. Raphael. Amen.

Try to avoid contact with the person who is trying to cling to you and especially do not receive food from her, because she can renew the spell through any food or drink.

SENTIMENTAL TIES

This type of spiritual coercion to appropriate the mind, heart and feelings of someone is elaborated in various ways, always taking something that represents the person you want to chain, such as a photo, a lock of hair, etc., and introducing it into an object that represents the part you want to affect: a doll if you want to bind the whole person, a chili or a cucumber if you want to bind the sexuality of a man, and an orchid or other flower that represents the sexuality of women. All this is usually tied with a red ribbon with seven knots, to which a magic incantation is added so that the binding takes effect.

Here we are particularly interested in concentrating on the meaning of the thread and the seven knots, which are the essence of this type of binding. The seven knots represent the seven chakras, which are the supposed energy centers of the human body, on which all energetic magic is based, especially acupuncture, and which are said to be associated with one of the endocrine glands of the physical body.

Esoteric beliefs state that the main functions of the chakras are to manage the body's moods by circulating vital energy, hence

101

destructive magics also attack these points to create depression and despair.

It is also stated that the chakras govern the self-awareness and psychological functions of people. This is one of the points that red magic seeks to subjugate to lessen the charge of conscience caused by marital infidelity, and to create the obsession that does not leave the affected person alone until he/she is in the hands of the one who elaborated or ordered the elaboration of the spell.

We can neither affirm nor deny the existence of the chakras, because theologically there is nothing described with which we can refute whether or not it is a spiritual reality or what in this esoteric language is called the point of contact of the soul with the body. What we can affirm is that in our arduous work of liberation we find that the focal points of spiritual contamination coincide with the points where the chakras are supposedly located. Suffice it to say here what we have said about them, as we will return to them in detail later when we talk about yellow magic.

I remember the case of a police officer who came to me because on the second day of marriage he had found a doll representing him hidden in one of his wife's drawers.

The doll was elaborated in the following way: on the outside it was wrapped with a green cloth representing his police uniform and tied to a white rope that had a specific number of knots that usually mean the potency of the human being that wants to bind the person who sends to do the job. Inside was a wax doll, to which they had pinned a lock of hair that the policeman identified as his own and which in turn were tied with a white ribbon, and this whole doll was wrapped with underwear fabric that the policeman also identified as his own.

The underwear means a sexual binding, with which it is wanted to reach the passionate obsession of the person towards the one who orders to elaborate the work; it goes without saying that the wax doll with the lock of hair is the personification of the victim to whom all these bonds and ties are transferred.

The gentleman, obviously, on his second day of his honeymoon was totally disappointed by the way they had used to coerce his sentimental inclinations towards the woman he had married, but it also made it clear to him why he had been forced to make the decision to marry in the short period of one month. This seemed too short of a time to all his relatives for him to make such a transcendental decision in a man's life.

With this example I only want to draw the attention of my readers to how these ties and bindings that witches offer in classified ads work. In this case it was a single man who was spiritually forced to make the decision to get married. But unfortunately, witchcraft is also used to attract and disorient the feelings and sexuality of married men and women, as we have already mentioned.

Our little faith does not allow us to glimpse the spiritual power that Satan has to manipulate the feelings and sexuality of human beings, as long as God allows it; but this divine permission is more common and frequent than many can imagine, since any act of superstition committed by the person or his ancestors gives Satan the key to work more and more at will over the human race.

Sexual binding could be defined as a kind of diabolical magnetism that affects the genital, sentimental and mental sensitivity of the person. This power of the demons over these human faculties dates from very ancient times; indeed, I would dare to say that since Adam and Eve themselves, since an analysis of the story of Genesis based on the punishments received by Adam and Eve after the first sin, one can reach the conclusion that behind the figure of the forbidden fruit could be found a sin of sexual type, that because of the modesty that the ancients had to deal with issues relating to sexuality was adorned under the figure of tasting a forbidden fruit and appetizing to the flesh.

The fact is that God is very just when it comes to imparting punishments and thus we see that the Lord in the course of the Holy Scriptures usually punishes in the same matter in which sin is committed. For example, David's adultery was punished by having Absalom, David's son, rape all his father's wives in broad daylight.

In the case of Adam and Eve, if they both committed the same sin of disobedience, there would be no reason to justify different punishments for them and in reality the only common punishment for both was death.

Adam is given as punishment the fatigues with which he was going to have to extract the fruits of the earth; but what attracts the attention of this reflection are the punishments that are given to the woman and that are intimately related to her sexual and sentimental life, that is to say: in Genesis 3, 16 "God says to the woman I will multiply your fatigues, as many as your pregnancies are, with pain you will give birth to your children". And the other punishment pronounced by the mouth of the Lord is: "your appetite shall go to your husband and he shall rule over you". If the sin had been to eat a fruit, I think that the most just punishment would have been this: "I will multiply the fatigue of your digestion and you will go to the bathroom with pain or in the best case that you will share with your husband the labors to take the sustenance from the earth".

According to the explanation that the Lord has given to some mystics, the sin of Eve consisted in the following: God had given them order and command to grow and multiply, but had reserved for a time giving them the knowledge of the manner in which fertilization was to be performed among them. The reason for this was that God was waiting for them to reach their full maturity, before revealing to them this mystery of love, for although they had been created in a state of bodily maturity, they were not yet intellectually mature, since the Lord wanted to instruct them with infused knowledge, little by little, about the different aspects of life.

Just as He was instilling in them knowledge about the different species of animals that He had created, Satan prompted Eve to detail how the animals reproduced among themselves, making her realize that she and her husband were also endowed with sexuality and the capacity for pleasure. The tempter persuades the woman not to wait for God's instruction on how they were to reproduce, but to go ahead and experience in herself that tasty fruit of sexual self-pleasure, and then invite her husband to copulate like the animals, and thus she would be like God in that she would have the ability to create other men whenever she and her husband pleased.

The Lord Jesus revealed to the mystics that the way God had arranged for human beings to reproduce was through an act of faith in God and mutual love, which, without the need for genital coparticipation, would engender children through a direct action of the Holy Spirit, as actually happened in the incarnation of the son of God. That is to say, that the way the Blessed Virgin Mary engendered and gave birth to Jesus Christ, without losing the innocence of the soul and the virginity of the body, would have been the usual way of perpetuating the human species if we had not sinned, therefore the way Jesus was born would not have been the exception to the rule but the rule itself.

This is not a doctrine of faith or dogma of the Church, but it is something that has helped me to understand why sexual disorders have been the hobbyhorse by which Satan has led so many souls to the loss of God.

If my readers want to accept for a moment this theory, in which God's plan was to make man a more spiritual being than a carnal being, and that precisely the works of the devil consist in upsetting this plan of spiritualization of man, to turn him into the worst and most carnal of beasts, then it will be possible to understand why Satan has so much power over our instinctive

105

feelings, and over our sexual pleasures, which was the point from which we started to make this biblical reflection of Genesis.

To my poor understanding, marriage is the least understood, least studied sacrament and will soon become the least desired. All this marriage-phobia has been uncultivated by Satan for years in our society, because he understands the power and importance of this sacrament. Marriage was used by St. Paul as an image of the union between Christ and the Church, and it is precisely this likeness that sanctifies the union between man and woman, as Christ was united and forms a single organism with his Church.

The sacrament makes the procreative act of man and woman obtain a sacred character, and therefore acquires, so to speak, a liturgical value. Let me explain: the sexual act, when sanctified by the sacrament of matrimony, goes from being an act that recalls before the eyes of God the ancient prevarication of Adam and Eve, to being a living reminder of the redemptive union between Christ and his mystical body: the Church.

What we have said implies that Christian spouses who have a higher view of faith could, and even should, offer their sexual acts to God with as much devotion as they would offer a fast or a prayer, since the Sacrament makes this act sacred.

Another of the most important values of the sacrament of marriage is that in it the spouses officiate the wedding as celebrants and not as assistants; that is to say, it is the only sacrament in which the priest is not the one who celebrates the sacrament, but is only a qualified witness that the Church places to give official character to the celebration, which in reality the spouses are doing. These, by virtue of the priesthood of the people of God, are the ones who act as priest and priestess who elaborate or make the sacrament of marriage, which they consummate on the first wedding night with their first sacred sexual act.

The sacrament of marriage then consecrates the husband and wife with a kind of priestly powers; whose faculties extend only to the spouses themselves and their offspring.

Hence, a father or a mother can bless their children and that blessing, in my opinion, has as much power as that of the priest, but only for their children, since this priestly marital power will not extend outside the members of the family that has been constituted through the sacrament of matrimony.

This is the most important point that I want to rescue, because this power that marriage gives to the spouses, empowers them to undo many diabolical influences that may be affecting the other spouse or their children.

Practically speaking, a person who is under the blessing of the sacrament of marriage could free a child from problems, for example drug addiction, alcoholism, rebellion, if he/she has enough faith, with a simple prayer. The following prayer is against drug addiction, alcoholism, rebellion:

In the name of our Lord Jesus Christ and by the power of the Sacrament of Matrimony, I expel from N.N. (mention the name of spouse or child you wish to release) any spirit of drug addiction or alcoholism or rebellion, and I command him/her to leave my home, sanctified by the Sacrament of Matrimony, and to no longer torment my family. And all this I decree in the name of God the Father Almighty, in the name of God the Son Redeemer of the world, in the name of God the Holy Spirit Defender, and by the power of binding and loosing which Holy Mother Catholic Church has, through the intercession of the most glorious ever Virgin Mary and through the ministry of the Holy Archangels St. Michael, St. Gabriel and St. Raphael. Amen.

Almost none of the Catholics understand the magnitude of the power that this sacrament gives them, and that together with that of the priesthood, they are the ones that can wreak the most havoc on the tyrannical empire of the devil. That is why Satan instigates his henchmen, the sorcerers and witches, to attack with all their malice and undermine these two sacraments, and they usually do so by means of the sexual binding of which we have spoken in other sections.

Care and treatment

As treatments against these bindings I propose to those men or women who are seeing their marital relationships affected by some intruder who tries to separate them to take possession of the feelings of their spouse, either with magical arts or without them, to try to reclaim the co-reason and the feelings of those loved ones, making use of the spiritual power that confers the sacrament of marriage, with a prayer like this one:

Prayer against marital division

In the name of Our Lord Jesus Christ and by virtue of the power of the sacrament of matrimony, I call for and claim the heart of my spouse N.N. and expel from my spouse's heart N.N. who attempts to separate what God has united.

In the name of Our Lord Jesus Christ and by virtue of the power of the sacrament of matrimony, I break every evil spell of marital division, sexual incompatibility and passionate infidelity.

I consecrate my home and my marriage to the custody of Jesus, Joseph and Mary, so that they may restore peace, love and fidelity to the home of Nazareth. Amen

For people who do not have the sacrament of marriage, what they should do if they are in concubinage is to put all their effort to sanctify their union through the sacrament. If it is a boyfriend or girlfriend, they should promise God that if the loved one is recovered, they will consecrate the relationship through the sacrament and then they will make the same prayer only that they will add to the phrase: "in the name of the sacrament of marriage that we are going to contract", thus, if the Lord sees that the intentions are right, he will listen to the prayer, and if not there will be no change in the attitudes of the person who we want to rescue.

Sexual bindings by Rituals

In order to make us realize the power that a witchdoctor can have and the danger to which many unwary women expose themselves when they lend themselves to do whatever these agents of evil suggest to them, I bring up a case I had to deal with in Argentina, where a woman desperate for a marriage division curse, thanks to which she saw her relationship with her husband more distant, went to a renowned witchdoctor begging him to undo the evil with which they were trying to separate her from her husband.

The sorcerer, seeing that the woman was beautiful, told her that he would try to undo the evil spell by giving her baths with herbs and potions, for which he asked her to take off all her clothes while he did the anointings and some strange prayers. After several sessions of these and upon hearing the woman complain that not only was the situation not improving, but it was getting worse, he assured her that the sexual binding she had was so strong, that could only be broken by a complex ritual, where he had to consecrate his semen and ejaculate inside her in order to break the binding.

Sadly, the woman was willing to do anything to get rid of this misfortune, but she did not know that precisely what the witchdoctor was doing was to ritualize her sexuality, so that from then on she would become his sexual toy.

109

This poor woman became the sexual slave of the witch-doctor, because according to her testimony, it was enough that he called her on the phone and she went out of her house like a zombie to go to copulate with that wretch, and although at first she did it with some repulsion, it ended up becoming a habit that lasted almost a year.

Fed up with this situation, she decided to go to a prayer group that was held in the cathedral of the city, and there began her ordeal, because when they made praises, she collapsed, losing consciousness and began to manifest diabolical presences, which with a male voice blasphemed in different languages. The priests of the cathedral, not knowing what to do with the poor woman, referred her to a priest of the Diocese who knew about exorcisms so that he could attend her. He, after attending to her in several sessions and seeing that there was no progress, decided to refer her to me. When I got my hands on her, I decided to do the deliverance together with her husband, because the Lord showed me that in this case, the witchdoctor had used copulation as a spell of consecration to Satan of this sexuality, priestly strength would not be enough to break this binding, but it would require that the husband, by virtue of the sacrament of matrimony, reclaim the sexuality and the body of his wife, and expel all the demons of lust that were possessing her.

Thanks to Our Lady and St. Joseph we were able to totally free the woman in a few sessions, because we concentrated the force of our attack on undoing the entrance door of the demons, through the force of the sacrament of marriage and not on spending force exorcising the demons that she had, as the previous exorcist had done, which would re-enter thanks to the sexual binding was not yet broken.

Care and treatment

For people who have undergone this type of rituals, they will first have to make the prayer of renunciation of witchcraft contained at the end of chapter II of this book.

If they let themselves be watered, they will proceed to undo it by sprinkling their body with exorcised water, mixed with a little exorcised salt, pronouncing the following prayer:

> *In the name of Our Lord Jesus Christ and by the power of the sacrament of baptism, signified in this water, I break, undo and dissolve any consecration, covenant or incantation that is affecting my body, my mind, my feelings or my sexuality, and I beseech Our Lord Jesus Christ to cleanse my whole being from the slime of Satan that may be contaminating me, in the name of God the Father Almighty, in the name of God the Son Redeemer of the world, in the name of God the Holy Spirit Defender, and by the power of the*
>
> *Holy Mother Catholic Church to bind and loose, through the intercession of the most glorious ever Virgin Mary and through the ministry of the Holy Archangels St. Michael, St. Gabriel and St. Raphael. Amen.*

We recommend that while the effects of this ritual last, you pray the following breaking prayer:

> *In the Name of Jesus Christ, the Lord, and by the merits of His precious blood, I break and dissolve every curse, hex, seal, spell, sorcery, witchcraft, bond, snare, trap, snare, ruse, lie, stumbling block, obstacle, de-ception, deviation, distraction, spiritual influence or chain, spirit of sleep that would obstruct my prayer; also every sickness of our body, soul and mind that can reach us, directly or through any person, animal or thing, or by any spirit that becomes present*

111

in us because of our own sins or mistakes, or those of our previous generations. Amen.

Chapter VI
Yellow magic

In some schools of witchcraft, yellow magic is associated by its color to gold and all that has to do with prosperity, which we already enclose everything in green magic. We prefer to associate it rather to illness and therefore it is closer to black magic than to white magic. The difference between yellow magic and black magic is that this magic seeks to cause in its victims diseases that lead them to despair, but without causing their death.

In this field we have come across a multitude of fictitious or imposed diseases, which although they have all the symptoms of a fatal disease, in reality doctors can never find any biological cause for such effects.

I remember a case in Argentina where witchcraft reduced a poor man to bed and although the doctors, after a multitude of examinations, determined that he was perfectly healthy, they gave up when they saw the man in a coma and his veins swelling with blood, without any cause in his cardiovascular tension or in any other diagnosable disease. Along the same lines we have come across people who have had psychiatric illnesses induced in order to get rid of them by seeing them confined in a mental hospital.

I particularly remember one lady who came to me in despair and told me that she thought she was crazy and that her children had already agreed to put her in a mental hospital the following Saturday. I told her to calm down because no crazy person thinks she is crazy; rather, believing that she is crazy is proof that she is psychically sane, and I proceeded to give her a prayer of deliverance where she quickly collapsed to the floor and the spiritual causes of this diabolical obsession were manifested. After the deliverance, this woman testified that we had saved her from spending the rest of her days in a mental institution and she told me this with tears of gratitude and joy.

I invite my readers to reflect on the number of people who may be confined in a psychiatric institution, deprived of their freedom because of a diabolical possession or an evil spell of derangement, and that with only a few prayers of deliverance or exorcism they could be reintegrated safe and sound into society and the love of their families.

With the above I do not mean to say that the experts in psychiatry and psychology are committing a fault by confining such people in a psychiatric clinic, because they cannot be required to believe in these realities, since their studies do not even speak to them of the possibility of such a reality; but what I do denounce is that priests and bishops should not interfere in the psychological and psychiatric field, which are not of their competence, but should attend only to the spiritual field, doing at least the minimum prayers to detect if the origin of such imbalance is diabolical or not, and in any case work hand in hand with experts in psychology and psychiatry in case it is a double origin, which can also occur where behind a psychic imbalance hides a diabolical possession. Moreover, I believe that all the most famous exorcists agree that even if a person has been diagnosed with a psychiatric illness, this should not stop him/her from practicing a prayer of exorcism, if he/she or his/her relatives ask for it, because as a Catholic psychiatrist friend told me, if the person is truly deranged, the prayer could never cause him/her any harm if the sick person asks for it. Rather, he will feel that God has not abandoned him in his sufferings, and above all, if the bishop and the priest are truly men of faith, they must admit that the psychiatric illness is not above the power of God, who is said in the Gospel to heal not only the demoniacs (Mark 5:15) but also the lunatics (Matthew 17:15).

HOW TO DETERMINE IF IT IS A PSYCHIATRIC ILLNESS OR POSSESSION

To show how easy it is to determine the origin of what appears to be a psychic disorder, I will narrate a personal experience.

A woman came to me saying that her nineteen year old son was showing certain signs of violence and behavior that seemed to her to be beyond the norm, and that sometimes he said that God was speaking to him and telling him doctrines that were too strange to be from our God, which made her suspect that it was a possible diabolical possession. But since she had consulted with her pastor and he had told her with certainty that it was a psychiatric illness and to take him for treatment, she had obeyed him. She had noticed that with the medications prescribed by the psychiatrist, the pseudomystical hallucinations and aggression had worsened. I then told her that the easiest way to tell if it was possession or illness was the following: to prepare the food that her son liked the most, using as part of its ingredients water, salt and oil, exorcised which are sacramentals of the Catholic Church, and I explained to her so that she would not believe that those elements were superstitious that water is a symbol of our baptism and that unlike holy water, which is to attract God's blessings, exorcised water has a special power to expel demons, since that is what the prayer that the priest prays over it is for. I also explained that the oil is a symbol of the anointing of the Holy Spirit with which the prophets, priests and kings were anointed since the Old Testament, and although the exorcised oil is different from the sacred oil consecrated by the bishop on Holy Thursday, in any case it has a special power given by the prayer that the priest makes over it to serve in the healing of diseases imposed by diabolical influences.

And finally I explained to him that the exorcised salt was already used since ancient times in the ritual of baptism in the part where Satan was exorcised from the catechumen, although later the rationalism of bishops and priests had tried to eliminate the use of this sacramental. I also explained to her that the power of the exorcised salt comes from the words of Christ: "you are the salt of the world..." (Mark 9, 50), where with the blessing of the priest the natural power that salt has to avoid the putrefaction of the flesh is elevated to supernatural, avoiding the presence of any satanic agent of corruption of man.

Thus instructed, I recommended her to be very attentive to the reaction of her son when he tasted this food so specially seasoned and to come and tell me the results. It did not take long for the good woman to appear again to tell me that her son, without having noticed the elements that she had put in his favorite food, unlike other occasions where he devoured it with anxiety, this time after the first spoonful he spat it out, throwing the plate on the floor and shouting at the woman that she wanted to poison him with such food.

Faced with such a reaction, I told the woman that there was no longer any doubt that it was a diabolical possession, since it is illogical to think that a psychiatric disease has the power to detect the presence of the sacramentals in a food that she had never refused.

To keep in mind

The diseases caused by witchcraft have the particularity of not being registered by medical examinations and tests, so that although the person feels all the effects of an illness, which should be caused by the malfunction of an organ, in reality that organ is perfectly healthy.

As we said when we talked about red magic, witch doctors usually use certain points of our organism where, according to them, our psychic and corporal health lies. Although they call them chakras, we will refrain from giving them any name, but we will limit ourselves to describe their position and the diseases that are linked, so that people who feel sick, despite being clinically healthy, seeing the places where they feel certain spiritual pricks, punctures or pains, without falling into hypochondria, can suspect that they are victims of an evil spell of yellow magic.

It should be noted that we should not always blame the devil for everything that happens to us, because there are also pains and even diseases that are caused by too high levels of stress. Let's start with the definition of these points.

First point

Also called root or base, located in the perineum, base of the spine (coccyx). Functions associated with it in the esoteric world: survival, physical vitality, creativity, abundance, instincts, self-preservation. Organs associated with it in the esoteric world: kidneys, bladder, spinal, suprarenals, colon, legs and bones.

If attacked by yellow magic it can cause the following deficiencies: unhealthy self-absorption, insecurity, uncontrollable anger or tendency to violence, excessive ambition, too much concern for what one will live on or for the future economic situation. When witchcraft affects a person of weak character and little faith, this can produce loss of vitality or the desire to live and even depressions.

When the person feels too much pain or tension in the spine and, as we said, after the necessary medical studies have been made, they do not find any affection that originates these contractions or pains in that point of the back, then he could suspect that some work is being done to make him lose his will to live or to fight. In this case it is not necessary to be alarmed nor to run to look for an exorcist, but it is enough that the faith is sufficiently robust to stop the diabolic action. In our days of deliverance, people with serious depression have come to us and the Lord has shown us that those who suffer from depression imposed by witchcraft present a tie along their entire spine that can be seen in different ways; for example, as a barbed wire that surrounds the entire spine or as staples that are nailed in certain parts of the back and that have their greatest concentration at the base of the spine that corresponds to the location of this root point or base that is in the coccyx.

We bless these people by anointing them with exorcised oil at that base point and also by making crosses along that depressive structure we make a prayer of breaking, until the Lord shows us that the evil spell of depression has been broken.

Many people have already testified that they have been totally healed of their depression or that at least the antidepressant medicines that had no effect before, after the breaking have begun to work.

Care and treatment

As we said before, you should proceed to anoint the affected parts with exorcised oil, making a small cross while repeating the following prayer:

> In the name of Our Lord Jesus Christ, I untie and destroy any witchcraft, sorcery or curse that is affecting these organs and I claim health in the name of the Blood of Christ that has washed us from our sins and I beseech Our God to restore the organs damaged by diabolical action, in the name of God the Father Almighty, in the name of God the Son Redeemer of the world, in the name of God the Holy Spirit Defender, and by the power of binding and loosing that Holy Mother Catholic Church has, through the intercession of the most glorious

ever Virgin Mary and through the ministry of the Holy
Archangels St. Michael, St. Gabriel and St. Raphael. Amen.

Sacral point

Located from the navel to the lower abdomen (one hand span below the navel). Functions associated with it in the esoteric world: procreation, assimilation of food, physical strength and vitality, center of sexual energy, center of sensations and emotions, sexuality.

Organs associated with it in the esoteric world: genitals, ovaries, testicles, prostate, spleen, belly and bladder.

When this point is attacked by yellow magic, it has as consequences sexual difficulties, uterine and/or urinary problems, excesses with food or sex, as well as confusion, jealousy, envy, desire for sexual possession, impotence, and so on.

As this point is mostly affected by blue magic, it will be seen in the following chapter, where we will give examples and describe how to proceed to make the break.

Solar plexus point

Located in the pit of the stomach. Functions associated with it in the esoteric world: center of power and wisdom, vitalizes the sympathetic nervous system, digestive processes, metabolism, emotions. Organs associated with it in the esoteric world: stomach, liver, gall bladder (digestive system), nervous system and muscles.

When this point is attacked by yellow magic, it causes digestive problems, bulimia and forced anorexia, chronic gastritis, ulcers, irritability of mood because of these diseases, malnutrition or abdominal swelling, without detectable physical cause and flatulence.

We have had to treat several people affected by bebedizos, which are spells inoculated through food or drink. We have noticed that when prayer is made on this point is when the desire to vomit from what has been eaten or drunk begins to manifest, In such a way that the person releases the food in which the potion was placed, even if there is no consumption of that type of food for days or even months, which implies that the food materializes again at the moment when the release is made.

Care and treatment

We recommend that in addition to the anointing and the prayer we mentioned in the first point, it is reinforced with the ingestion of a little exorcised water to speed up the process of expulsion of the drink, while the following prayer is said:

> *In the name of Our Lord Jesus Christ, by the power of the sacrament of baptism signified in this water that I am about to drink, may all my bowels be cleansed of any diabolical incursion that would affect the health of my mind, my body or my soul, may all the bonds of sin and evil that are binding me by the most precious passion be broken, death and resurrection of Our Lord Jesus Christ and this be done in the name of God the Father Almighty, in the name of God the Son Redeemer of the world, in the name of God the Holy Spirit Defender, and by the power of the Holy Mother Catholic Church to bind and loose, through the intercession of the most glorious ever Virgin Mary and through the ministry of the Holy Archangels St. Michael, St. Gabriel and St. Raphael. Amen.*

Cordial point

Located in the center of the chest. Functions associated with it in the esoteric world: preserves the vital force, gives energy to the body and governs the circulation of the blood.

Organs associated with it in the esoteric world: heart, circulatory system, arms, hands and lungs.

When this point is attacked by yellow magic, it produces stagnation of feelings, emotional imbalances, as well as circulatory and cardiac problems.

People have come to us who have felt a violent change in their attitudes towards their loved ones, and after checking their hormone levels and doing psychological therapies have not found a solution to these changes, from being very affectionate to be aggressive, even to feel repulsion towards loved ones such as parents, spouse, children.

After analyzing that it was not a problem of inner healing (sequels that are left by some disorders or mistreatment suffered from the mother's womb, in childbirth, in childhood, in puberty of the person), confirming that it was not possible to find a physical, psychological or spiritual cause for such changes, then we proceeded to do the prayer of liberation where we discovered a tie of yellow magic at this level, we proceeded to break it and people returned to their usual state of mind.

It should be noted that this change of mood is not necessarily caused by a yellow magic spell, but may also have its origin in a curse as will be seen in the later chapters.

Throat point

Located in the neck area, as it affects not only the throat but also the back of the neck. Functions associated with it in the esoteric world: communication, expression, clairvoyance, speech, sound, vibration. Organs that associate him in the esoteric world: throat, lungs, thyroid, parathyroid, hypothalamus and mouth.

When this point is attacked by yellow magic, it causes communication problems that, although the person feels that he speaks perfectly, other people have difficulty understanding what he wants to express, especially the people who are under his charge and who must follow his instructions. Also, in some severe cases, pronunciation problems may occur. It can also affect the capacity for discernment and clarity in evaluating situations, and this point can also be associated with the depressive structure that we spoke of earlier, but not in terms of tiredness, sadness and discouragement, but in terms of negative and obsessive ideas of contempt for life, and it can also cause thyroid problems. In the spiritual field we have noticed that people who have charismas of the Holy Spirit, when the sorcerers block them, they use that point but in the base of the neck.

The most typical example we have found for this type of spiritual attack is when people are affected in their capacity of concentration and assimilation, especially in students who are blocked by their schoolmates out of envy in order to annul them and surpass their averages. In this case, sometimes it is not even necessary a curse itself, but it is enough with an act of sending or a curse to unleash the diabolical action.

Care and treatment

We recommend sealing these points with exorcised oil before entering places where you feel this type of blockage; for example, office, classroom, library, etc., using a sealing formula like the following:

> With the Holy Blood of Jesus, I cover, we cover, and seal this place, our homes, our house or apartment, all those who dwell in them... (name), the people whom the Lord will send to them, all our loved ones wherever they may be and their homes, friends, neighbors, coworkers, our belongings, doors, windows, objects, walls, floors, all corners of the house, ceilings, pipes, drains, household items and work materials, utensils, artwork and religious images, plants, books,

122

evangelization materials; our moments of prayer, rest, healthy entertainment, our sleep, the air we breathe, domestic or pest animals present in this place or in our homes, as well as the food and goods that He generously sends us for our sustenance, and in faith we place a circle of the precious Blood of the Lord Jesus.

With the Holy Blood of Jesus, I cover, we cover, and seal the places where we will be today, the individuals, companies, or institutions we will interact with... (names), likewise, we cover and seal our material and spiritual work, business, studies, highways, airways, roads, automobiles, and any means of transportation we will use. We break any satanic influence that may be in our minds, in our tongues, in our memories, in our ability to communicate, and we ask our Lord for His Holy Spirit to guide our words and actions so that we do not deviate from His will, through Jesus Christ our Lord. Amen.

Frontal Point

Located in the center of the forehead, between the eyebrows. Functions associated with it in the esoteric world: vitalizing the lower brain (cerebellum and central nervous system), vision, the center of intuition, seat of willpower and clairvoyance. Organs associated with it in the esoteric world: sympathetic nervous system, hypothalamus, pituitary gland, left eye, nose, and ears. If it is under attack by yellow magic, it can cause the following deficiencies: lack of concentration, fear, cynicism, tension, headaches, eye problems, nightmares, indifference towards life.

It is common to find people who suffer from migraines and strange head pains that have no medical explanation and cannot be controlled with any strong analgesics. In such cases, after performing the liberation, we ask them to inform their doctors that they have stopped experiencing the pain and that the medicine used is exorcised oil and a few breaking prayers, such as the one we have already mentioned in Chapter IV of red magic.

Crown Point

Located at the crown of the head. Functions associated with it in the esoteric world: vitalizing the upper brain and unifying spiritual activities.

Organs associated with it in the esoteric world: endocrine system, pineal gland, cerebral cortex, central nervous system, and the right eye.

When this point is under attack by yellow magic, it causes a lack of inspiration, confusion, depression, difficulty in praying and carrying out devotions, and a diminished willingness to serve, premature aging.

We have encountered cases of individuals with a strong spiritual life, even leading prayer groups, who suddenly lost all their enthusiasm for the work of God and found it increasingly difficult to engage in their devotional practices. In the liberations, the Lord revealed to us that they had been attacked by witches who infiltrate Catholic prayer groups to hinder the work of God and, in a sense, drain the charisms of God's servants. Obviously, after breaking this binding, they returned to their normal state.

Care and Treatments

We recommend that the person anoints the crown of their head with oil, lays hands on themselves, and recites the following prayer:

In the name of our Lord Jesus Christ, I break every diabolic oppression that may be in my mind, in my head, in my eyes, and in all my understanding. I also break every diabolic oppression that seeks to bind my faculties, which I consecrate to the service of our God and Lord, the Father of Jesus Christ

124

our Lord. In faith, I put on His armor, I gird myself with the belt of truth and the helmet of salvation. I take up the shield of faith to extinguish the fiery darts of the devil, and I wield the sword of the Holy Spirit, which is the Word of God.

To conclude this chapter, I want to warn all individuals that they should refrain from closing their chakras, thinking that by doing so they will avoid the effects of witchcraft. In reality, they are closing themselves off to God's graces and the work of the Holy Spirit. Similarly, they should abstain from allowing themselves to be manipulated through Reiki and chakras. As we have seen, Reiki falls within the realm of white magic and therefore cannot be blessed by God. Furthermore, the person practicing Reiki absorbs all the spiritual contamination from their clients, which as mentioned earlier, often leads to the loss of their own health and even contaminates others.

In the event that the chakras have been mistakenly closed, the individual can reopen them by anointing themselves with exorcised oil and reciting the following prayer:

May the Blood of Jesus restore my entire being to its original state and dissolve any binding that ignorance and superstition may have caused in me. By the power of binding and loosing bestowed upon the Church, I decree that my soul, body, and spirit are returned to the state of freedom as children of God. I declare this in the name of Almighty God the Father, in the name of God the Son, the Redeemer of the world, in the name of God the Holy Spirit, the Defender, and through the power of binding and loosing held by the Holy Catholic Church. I seek the intercession of the most glorious Virgin Mary and invoke the ministry of the Archangels St. Michael, St. Gabriel, and St. Raphael. Amen.

Chapter VII

Blue magic

Like other forms of magic, blue magic has various branches. One branch is aligned with white magic and encompasses the search for arcane knowledge and the spiritual and mental powers that supposedly are not developed by the common person, but only by those who undertake the task of tapping into those hidden powers within our being. The other branch leans towards black magic and could be considered a combination of red and black magic, which we will discuss further later on.

VARIETIES OF BLUE MAGIC

Mind Control

This type of magic tries to influence positively or negatively on the beliefs and thoughts of other people, exercising spiritual coercion through a gaze, which will limit the decisions or opinions of the person being influenced by this type of magic.

Some of the abilities that this aspect of blue magic aims to develop are related to the capacity to perceive different forms of spiritual manifestations, which they believe reside in the intuition of the mind and can be more or less developed depending on the individual and their inherent talents. Some of these phenomena include:

Clairvoyance

Clairvoyance is the ability to see spiritual things, including future events. It is believed that this ability is accompanied by the capacity to provide precise solutions to each problem. This esoteric capacity of clairvoyance has its counterpart within the Catholic religion in the charismatic gifts of vision and prophecy. Therefore, we could say that clairvoyance is an anti-charism received directly from dark forces. Hence, we affirm that there is no need to resort to these arts to develop these abilities since our God freely grants them to those who ask for them.

Clairaudience

According to esotericism, clairaudience is the ability to hear the thoughts of other people or to clearly understand what spiritual entities want to communicate. Similar to the previous ability, clairaudience has its counterpart within the charisms of the Holy Spirit, known as spiritual hearing. This gift allows servants of God to hear the inspirations of the Holy Spirit and to receive messages from saints, angels, or souls in purgatory. Examples include St. Gemma, who could hear her guardian angel, or Padre Pio, who had conversations with Jesus and the Virgin Mary, among others. Once again, it is important to emphasize that Satan is like a chimpanzee imitating God in all His works. Seeing that God grants charisms to His servants, Satan also grants opposing gifts to his slaves, the witches.

Clarisentency

Esoterically it is understood as experiencing a positive or negative reaction to a situation of which you have no previous evaluation. It is like an intuitive inspiration that predisposes you in favor or against certain people. It is very similar to what in popular language has been called feminine intuition. It has its antagonist within the Catholic Charismatic Renewal in the charisms of word of wisdom, word of knowledge and divine inspiration.

Auric sense

According to esoteric language, it is the ability to perceive the magnetic ring that surrounds all objects, beings and emotions, which according to them is what makes a person inspire trust and sympathy, or the opposite.

This satanic anti-charisma has no equivalent in what the Holy Spirit gives, since God does not like us to judge by appearances or intuitions but to give the opportunity to people by their actions, since He tells us "by their fruits you will know them".

Telepathy

It is the ability to exchange thoughts without the need to use words or gestures. Unfortunately it is used in mind control to sneak thoughts into the mind of another person against their will. It is a satanic anti-charisma, since God does not like us to violate the freedom of others. It is not even recommended when it is done between two people who want to communicate through telepathy, since this implies opening the levels of subconsciousness to a dangerous degree where a diabolical entity can easily intervene and give us what we call satanic obsession.

Evil eye

It is the ability of some evil people to pro-duce a spiritual evil through their gaze. We put it within the arts of blue magic, since it is required to do this type of damage of acquired or inherited mental power. It is very common to think that only sorcerers can remove it, but in reality any child of God can undo the evil eye with a prayer as simple as the one that appears in the Holy Scripture in Numbers 6, 22-27:

May the Lord bless you and keep you; may the Lord shine upon you and be gracious to you; may the Lord show his face to you and give you peace. Amen.

On one occasion, my brother took me to do prayer at his workplace and told me that his boss had let him in charge of me to enter his office so we could pray and see what the Lord showed us.

As soon as we entered her office, the Lord showed us that they were doing blue magic on her through mind control. When my brother found out he insisted that we call her to tell her. He put her on the phone, before telling her anything I asked her if when she was at home or out of the office she made even drastic decisions such as firing or reprimanding any of her employees and when she arrived at the office she immediately changed her mind, thinking that the decision would be too extreme. The surprised woman said that this was exactly what happened to her, and not just once, but on many occasions. Then we recommended her to seal her forehead with exorcised oil before entering her office and to do the exercise of continuing with the decisions she made outside the office and to try not to make any while she was in the office, until she could get rid of the people she detected were the ones who were doing this type of witchcraft to her.

Care and treatment

People who feel and believe that they are victims of mind control, we recommend anointing themselves with oil by making a cross on their forehead and reciting the following prayer:

Jesus lives, Jesus rules, Jesus reigns in my mind, and in His name we block and undo all mental control that is being done to me, and I consecrate my thoughts and my decisions to the

129

Holy Spirit so that He alone may inspire and govern me, for the duration of my pilgrimage on this earth, through Jesus Christ Our Lord. Amen.

THE BRANCH THAT LEANS TOWARDS BLACK MAGIC

In this aspect of blue magic, we could say that it is a combination of red magic (sexual) and black magic (malefic), which aims to cause destructive disturbances at a sexual level.

Its effects range from causing sexual impotence in men to developing all the symptoms of venereal diseases without the presence of the disease-causing bacteria. Naturally, these symptoms do not improve with antibiotic treatment but do improve with the use of sacramentals. In the case of women, this type of magic attacks the sources of a woman's vanity, causing breast cancer, vaginal hemorrhages that hinder a healthy sexual life with their spouses, uterine or ovarian cancer leading to infertility, and in some cases, inducing excessive or disproportionate obesity despite the amount of food consumed.

Personally, we have encountered several cases of men who, as payment for their emotional disorders, have received as a gift from their former lovers testicular pain that not only hinders their normal sexual life but also intensifies significantly during moments of prayer and especially during Holy Mass. These types of bindings have been conjured by the women who felt deceived by them, not only to prevent the man from having another sexual partner besides her but also to hinder any form of a fulfilling life with such discomfort and pain.

Particularly in one of these cases we attended to, this spiritual contamination was contracted by visiting brothels, and this is where we need to discuss what is called ritual prostitution. This type of prostitution treats this work as a sort of religion, where each woman

130

is subjected to certain rituals in which the witch covers them with incense, bathes them with herbal washes, anoints them with essences, and consecrates them to a spirit of lust. As a result, any man who has sexual relations with them acquires such sexual contamination that can only be satisfied through their aberrant desires with the prostitutes in that establishment. If they attempt to distance themselves from that life and convert to a life of piety, as in the case we are still addressing, attending any prayer group or Holy Mass will cause indescribable genital torment. It requires a great deal of willpower and determination to endure such suffering and not return to their former life of sin.

Care and Treatment:

In these cases, the same approach described when addressing the malefic effects of red magic will be followed. The only difference here compared to that type of magic is that in this genre of malefic effects, the assistance of an exorcist priest will be needed because these types of consecrations are performed by a satanic priest. Therefore, the priestly power is required to undo their works.

In Chapter V on Red Magic, look for an Exorcist Priest and ask to help you by doing the following breaking:

Prayer to be said by the priest

In the name of our Lord Jesus Christ and the priestly power conferred upon me by the Holy Mother Catholic Church, using the faculty of binding and loosing, I break, shatter, and dissolve all sexual binding, all consecration and covenant with spirits of lust, and cleanse all spiritual contamination that this child of God has contracted through their sins or the sins of their ancestors, or through envy, curse, or hex effects of their enemies. I decree this in the name of Almighty God the Father, in the name of God the Son, the Redeemer of the

world, in the name of God the Holy Spirit, the Defender, and
through the power of binding and loosing held by the Holy
Mother Catholic Church. I seek the intercession of the most
glorious Virgin Mary and invoke the ministry of the
Archangels St. Michael, St. Gabriel, and St. Raphael. Amen.

Binding of Sterility and Impotence

Another wickedness devised by this type of magic is to cause sterility and impotence in its victims. As mentioned before, it can also create an appearance of venereal diseases that lead spouses to consider separating from the affected person. This can be due to the inability to conceive children or the disgust caused by the eruptions, sores, or discoloration of the genitals, which, although inexplicable to medical professionals, appear as if under infection.

Numerous young women also fall victim to this kind of wickedness, developing breast cancer at an age when doctors would typically refuse to perform mammograms. The perpetrators derive pleasure from causing these women to suffer through the amputation of their breasts. Similarly, there is an increasing prevalence of cancers of the uterus, ovaries, and prostate, which have no hereditary or biological explanation for their origin.

A young married couple came to us after struggling for ten years to conceive. They had exhausted all methods of artificial conception and were on the verge of accepting the need to adopt a child when they approached us for help.

During our prayer for them, we immediately detected a bond of blue magic that was spiritually causing their infertility. This explained why the doctors, based on their assessments, deemed them perfectly capable of having children, yet they could not conceive. We proceeded with the breaking prayer and asked them to reinforce it with the prayer against marital division, which we have mentioned at the end of Chapter V. One month later, they called us with the good news that the wife was pregnant. To this date, five children have been born thanks to these prayers we have conducted.

Care and treatment

In these types of cases, the assistance of an exorcist priest is indeed necessary to perform the breaking prayer. The procedure would be as follows:

- Both prepare themselves for nine days by praying to each other the prayer that we put in chapter V of breaking the evil spell of marital division.
- After these nine days of prayer, they will make the renewal of the marriage vows as it appears at the beginning of chapter V, preferably in the presence of the exorcist priest who will perform the deliverance.

Prayer for breaking the binding of sterility or sexual disease, to be pronounced by the priest:

In the name of our Lord Jesus Christ and the priestly power conferred upon me by the Holy Mother Catholic Church, using the faculty of binding and loosing, I break, shatter, and dissolve all sexual binding and sterility that hinder the work of the God of life, so that these children of God may fulfill the command of their Creator: "Be fruitful and multiply."

Furthermore, I break and undo every hex of genital disease, prostate, ovaries, uterus, or breasts that has been caused by the wickedness of Satan's agents. I command that, by the mercy of God, all organs damaged by these envies, curses, or hexes effects be restored. I decree this in the name of Almighty God the Father, in the name of God the Son, the Redeemer of the world, in the name of God the Holy Spirit, the Defender, and through the power of binding and loosing held by the

Holy Mother Catholic Church. I seek the intercession of the most glorious Virgin Mary and invoke the ministry of the Archangels St. Michael, St. Gabriel, and St. Raphael. Amen.

MAGICAL OBJECTS THAT WE DO NOT RECOMMEND HAVING AT HOME

Before moving on to black magic, we would like to dedicate a few paragraphs to warn about some other esoteric elements that although they do not belong exclusively to blue magic, they are present in it and in all other magics, including black magic.

- *Elephant.* This animal is considered divine by some religions, but esoterics believe that it attracts money and abundance to the home, therefore it will actually cause God to withdraw his blessings.

- *Horseshoe.* They say that putting it on the door of the house prevents the entry of negative energies and attracts luck, they even go to the extreme of asking to touch it or hold it in your hand for a moment during the day to promote energy renewal. In reality, an apparently innocent object like this contains a whole apocalyptic symbolism of those horsemen of extermination, who used the different horses as a symbol of the plagues and punishments of God. That is why we ask all people not to have these items in their homes, because they actually work as a talisman and attract the diabolic presence and open the door of our homes wide open.

- *Quartz.* They are supposed to channel energies and it is very common to find them in the form of prisms or pyramids. Different powers are attributed to them according to their colors. In reality, these stones and many other metals and precious stones belong to the magic of the earth and stones, and get their power from the place where they were extracted, since the obscurantist tradition says that when they

134

were buried in the depths they absorb the magical powers of hell.

- *Chinese lucky cat.* It is a golden cat that moves its little hand and supposedly attracts wealth and customers to businesses. It actually belongs to Chinese magic and, as we all know, the cat has always been an element present in all potions and spells. We also recommend refraining from having elements with Chinese letters, as we have noticed that many of them contain pacts, consecrations and invocations.

- *Egyptian papyri.* It has become a fashion to decorate houses with Egyptian effigies, manuscripts and hieroglyphics. We remind our readers that Egyptian magic was the origin of the so feared gypsy magic; therefore, to have all those symbols, whose meanings we do not know, is to risk having in reality incantations and pacts with those pagan gods of death that the Egyptians worshipped, whom our God so harshly punished with plagues.

- *Old keys.* Supposedly they are used to keep the roads open and to keep money, work, love and luck flowing into our home. In reality, the key has a great magical symbolism, because in witchcraft it is used to open the interdimensional doors that give the entrance to our world to the infernal legions. That is why in most movies where magic is discussed, a key is always sought to give people access to the esoteric worlds.

- *Colored candles.* Candle magic is one of the most commonly practiced forms of magic due to its simplicity. Different colored candles are used according to the days of the week, each associated with a magical power ranging from cleansing, protection, angelic invocation, love, prosperity, health, energy renewal, relaxation, to extreme effects such as warding off enemies, removing witchcraft, warding off the evil eye, and spiritual communication with the beyond.

Therefore, we recommend abstaining from using colored candles as they may already be consecrated from the factory to produce the attributed magical effects. God cannot be involved in these superstitions and witchcraft, and thus any effects achieved through the superstitious use of colored candles can only be attributed to the power of the devil.

For faithful individuals who like to accompany their prayers to God by lighting a candle, it is recommended to ensure that the candle does not have any esoteric symbols embossed in the wax or printed on the labels, such as the yin and yang symbol, the five-pointed star, the Egyptian death cross with a horseshoe-like shape instead of the upper crossbar, or other non-Christian symbols, including Chinese characters. It is also recommended that the candles they use be blessed by a priest or be consecrated during the Easter Vigil or Candlemas.

Before entering the dark realm of black magic, we must clarify that in some witchcraft schools, there is also what is called pink magic and gray magic. We won't dedicate a separate chapter to these types of magic, as pink magic essentially falls under red magic, as we mentioned earlier, focusing on blood magic, while pink magic encompasses all aspects of love magic. On the other hand, gray magic is the portion of blue magic that, as we previously mentioned, leans towards black magic, and they claim it lies between white and black magic. They argue that their spells are not as beneficial as white magic but also not as malevolent as black magic.

Chapter VIII
Black magic

It is properly evil magic, that is, the one whose sole purpose is to cause evil in a person, but above all things seeks to induce death in any way possible. Among the evil spells that are performed in this type of magic, the ones we have encountered the most in our work are those that we call extreme depression, which seek to eliminate the person by inducing a catastrophic state of mind with the intention of inducing death by any kind of suicide.

Also as we have said in previous chapters, there is the curse of anorexia induced in such a way that it creates in the person such an inappetence that leads to the brink of death, and this not by vanity as normally happens in the disease of bulimia and anorexia, but by physical repugnance to eat or because every time food is ingested it causes in the person the opposite effect; that is to say, instead of gaining weight, the person dries up, since the food is not assimilated and causes stomach pains and medically unexplainable diarrhea.

Also the famous "burials" are characteristic of this type of magic and consist in taking objects that belong and represent the person who is to be harmed. They are buried in a grave of someone who has died in an accident or preferably has been murdered, making a spell so that the soul in pain of the deceased transfers his misfortune on the person to whom you want to do evil.

We priests are not always victorious in the fight against this type of witchcraft, as I still remember, and not without shock, the case of a woman whom I had to follow up with several deliverance sessions, and thanks to this type of witchcraft caused her such an intestinal infection and such physical weakening, that not only reduced her to crutches, but even caused her death. My only consolation was the message she sent me from her deathbed, since I was out of the country at the time she passed to a better life and whose message said more or less as follows: "Father Juan, I thank you from my heart because you were the only priest who believed me, who truly committed himself to my suffering, and although it was not God's will that he could free me, the only thing I can assure you is that from wherever I am, you will have in me an eternal intercessor to continue with your vocation and ministry".

VARIETIES OF BLACK MAGIC

Voodoo

This type of black magic has its origin in the pagan religions coming from West Africa, from where slaves were captured and then taken to populate from North America to South America. This pagan pseudo-religion has its most important centers in Cuba, Haiti and Brazil. In Cuba it originated the Cuban Santeria or the Regla de Ocha. Regarding Haiti, it is even said that at some time in the 18th century it was proclaimed as the official religion of the country by the reigning government and, in my opinion, it is the cause of the wrath of God that unleashed the earthquake that struck the country some time ago. As for Brazil, it has originated one of the satanic sects that is catalogued worldwide as the most effective in its evil spells, which is called Umbanda. Likewise, it also originated in Brazil other sects such as candomble and kimbanda.

Voodoo, in all its forms, consists of a mixture of African Paganism and Christianity, which leads to Santeria where they assign a pagan divinity or loas to each Catholic saint, and that is what has led so many unsuspecting Catholics to think that this is something good and not a satanic sect.

Voodoo rites are quite macabre, including animal and sometimes human sacrifices. It is attributed with the ability to manufacture zombies to put them to work in their favor, they also have the ability to cause death at will. Their fame has extended to literature and the seventh art with their famous dolls with which they cause the damage caused to the doll to be transferred to the person it represents.

Regarding the etymological meaning of the word voodoo, the criteria do not manage to agree because some say it means omnipresent magic, others make it derive from French words such as vaudois which means sorcery or vaudoux which means black sorcerer.

Goetia

Its name comes from a Greek word that meant sorcery or witchcraft. This type of black magic is mainly based on the invocation and evocation of demons, because, according to them, demons awaken love and destroy enemies, grant power and honor and are good teachers and tutors, they also give the ability to know the past, present and future. In addition, to those who practice it, they assign some minor demons that they call familiars, which are like a kind of guardian demons.

Solomonic magic

This type of black magic is based on books that claim to have been written by King Solomon, which is an obvious deception by Satan. The most famous of them are The Lesser Key of Solomon or the Lemegeton. They are supposedly based on the wisdom King Solomon received to control legions of spirits.

Not even those who practice this type of magic believe that King Solomon was the author of this book, since the most antique versions date from the 16th century and the magic contained therein is closely related to Babylonian magic. These books contain a long list of demons and rulers of darkness, they even speak of androgynous demons, which is why Solomonic magic is also used by the goetic.

Satanic sects

Among the black magics, if I may say so, the blackest of all is the one that comes from the satanic sects, which have liturgies opposed to that of the Catholic Church, where they have their anti-sacraments ranging from the rite of initiation, which is like an anti-baptism, where the salvation of Jesus Christ is renounced and the soul is sold to Satan; passing through the satanic marriage, where the man and the woman propose to live according to the seven deadly sins; reaching the satanic priesthood that empowers them to celebrate or direct the dreaded red or sexual masses and the black or destructive masses, of which many demonologists have written in their books and therefore I am not going to dwell here on the description of the rituals, but on their effects.

Just as we Catholics have a holy mass celebrated to obtain a grace from God, so do Satanic priests offer their black masses to cause harm, ruin or death to people. There are three extremely perverse elements of the black mass, which are the ones that unleash the restraints with which God has usually bound Satan, they are the following:

- *Rape of children under five years of age*, which are abused during the ritual. The loss of the innocence of these creatures empowers Satan to intervene harmfully in the sexuality of those for whom the black mass is offered.
- *The introduction of the consecrated* host inside the genitals of a naked woman who serves as an altar, to be thrown to the ground and trampled by all participants. This gives

Satan the power to destroy the faith of the person to be harmed.

- *The murder of the children or of the young girl* which has served as an altar, if still a virgin, and then eat their flesh and drink their blood while they remain lukewarm, by all those who participate in the black mass, as a parody of Catholic communion. The purpose of this act is to renounce communion with the spiritual and bodily presence of Christ in the Eucharist in order to exchange it for sacrilegious communion with the flesh and blood of the victims, symbols of lust and the passions of the flesh. This part of the ceremony empowers Satan to end the life of the person for whom the mass has been commanded to be celebrated. Although we could speak of other rituals of the satanic sects, such as the suffocation, among others, we will not dwell on them, because as it is obvious, the most pernicious of all is the black mass. I want to conclude this description of the worst sources of black magic by saying that we cannot be too alarmed, because the action of Satan is always restricted by divine authority, and although we should not underestimate the power of these spells to leave them unattended, thinking that because we are people of prayer "they will not affect us"... Must be translated into the reality that the consequences will not be as dire as these agents of evil would like, but they can certainly disrupt our spiritual life, our health and our economy to a greater or lesser degree, as God allows so that we begin to believe and defend ourselves from these evils.

While I was in Rosario, Argentina, I was approached by a pious woman whom I was directing spiritually, asking me to help her because she was desperate due to thoughts of suicide and the desire to end her own life, which had appeared a couple of months

141

ago and had worsened to such an extent that they already seemed unbearable to her.

I proceeded to say a few prayers of liberation over the lady's forehead, expelling any spirit of suicide, despair or depression, and instantly the woman felt healed and liberated and went home happy. What I did not expect was that minutes later she called me to tell me that she felt the same as at the beginning, from the moment she entered her house. Since she was in imminent danger of death, I told her not to move from there, while I arrived with some of my servants of the Lord who had charismas of sensibility, to detect the place where the source of the evil spells could be, and that in the meantime she should pray prayers of consecration of her life to Jesus and of rejection of all thoughts of death while we arrived.

The fact was that we searched the house from top to bottom, and apart from finding a general contamination, which should disappear with a prayer of deliverance and the use of the sacramentals, we did not see any source that we could suspect of producing such disturbances in the mind of this pious lady.

When I asked her to recall where these negative thoughts and feelings were most intense, she declared to us that it was while she was trying to sleep in her bed. I sent my servants of the Lord to check the mattress, the pillows and, oh surprise, when one of them touched an old suitcase that the lady had with clothes under her bed, this servant of the Lord immediately had to leave to vomit because of the spiritual contamination contained in that object. We asked her what she kept there besides those useless old clothes and she answered me surprised that she used it as a kind of safe to keep the money coming from some rents.

When she took out the money and passed it to me, I could not stand the burning in my hands and my servants of the Lord felt uncontrollable nausea when approaching it, so we told the lady that we had no doubt that this money was the source of her misfortunes. She opened her eyes as if the whole mystery had become clear to her and told us that just two months ago, when these thoughts began to appear, it was when some conflictive tenants who I had wanted to get away from, because of the problems they were giving her, had mysteriously decided to stop depositing the rent in the bank, to give it to her personally and in cash. Of course, she explained that the intention of these evil people was to induce her to commit suicide in order to keep the property that belonged to her, since she had no relatives to inherit it.

I believe that with this example it is sufficiently clear that the malice of men has no limit and that it is we Catholics who are behind in the field of faith, that is why we are helpless victims against these scoundrels who decimate the flock of God without anyone doing anything to prevent it. Now more than ever we live that reality that Jesus Christ said, "I send you out as sheep in the midst of wolves", for He well knew that in these last times most of the shepherds were going to be mercenaries who are not willing to give their lives for their flock.

Care and treatment

The first thing to consider is how to determine that we are under a black magic spell. For this purpose, we will use the indicators of the influence of black magic:

- People who are prayerful will begin to feel aversion towards liturgical acts, especially the Holy Mass.
- The moment of communion is no longer a special moment of encounter with Christ, but a moment of discomfort, of conflicting thoughts and even hallucinations that incite blasphemy.
- Loss of consciousness in moments of strong praise and worship with manifestations of violence or blasphemy, which do not remain in memory when one comes to oneself.

143

- Repudiation or repulsion against the Blessed Virgin Mary or extreme indisposition to pray the holy rosary.
- Ghoulish nightmares that incite attempts on your life or the lives of others.
- Perceiving spiritual presences in your home or place of work, which make physical manifestations such as turning on lights, start the car, turn on the TV or move things around.
- Being touched or physically or sexually assaulted by an evil entity.

Here are some treatments to counteract black magic:
- Once you have detected that you are under the influence of one of these black magic spells, you must counteract the evil thoughts that inspire you by continuous acts of faith, hope and charity. How to: *My God, I believe, adore, hope and love you, and I ask your forgiveness for those who do not believe, adore, hope and love you. Strengthen my faith to face the spiritual battles and temptations with which the evil one surrounds me.*
- To take refuge in the Eucharist and the Holy Rosary, even if one feels nothing.
- To have recourse to an exorcist priest for a prayer of deliverance or an exorcism, as he sees fit.
- In case of not being able to get an exorcism, no matter how desperate we may be, we should never resort to any witch-doctor. This will only make the situation worse because it will lead us further away from God, who is our only refuge. In the last case, you can look for a prayer group of the Catholic Charismatic Renewal, whose directors know how to make prayers of deliverance.
- In the most desperate of cases in which you cannot count on any of the spiritual aids that the Holy Mother Catholic

Church has, look for the exorcism of Leo XIII and pray it in the family, with the faith that God will never stop listening to his sheep. Knowing that this exorcism was written by this supreme pontiff for the laity to defend themselves from satanic oppressions, therefore, although there are some writings and decrees that ecclesiastical Freemasonry has distributed to put fear in people not to practice this prayer of liberation, it must be said that no ecclesiastical authority can put itself above the authority of a supreme pontiff and if Pope Leo XIII destined it for the use of the faithful, no one on earth has the authority to change that will.

Chapter IX
Other Spiritual Threats

The spiritual world is a reality too wide to be exhausted in a single book, but as we wanted to make this manual as complete as possible so that people of faith can give a logical and spiritual explanation to their ailments, and so they can give faster solutions to the ailments that maybe they suffer for a long time, without seeing any improvement despite all their prayers and prayers.

That is why we want to bring in this chapter, with other points of spiritual contamination that have as much or greater power than witchcraft itself and that unfortunately are very little considered and combative by people of prayer.

CURSES AND BLESSINGS

Another important topic that we should talk about and that is of utmost importance, is about the power that curses and blessings have to affect the lives of human beings.

The strength and power of the blessing is testified in different passages of the Holy Scriptures, especially in Genesis, where it is declared that the blessing that parents gave to their children were of vital importance to them. So much so, that even the brothers come to fight to receive the blessing of their dying father, as in the case of Genesis 27, 30, where Jacob with his wiles manages to receive from his father Isaac, the blessing that his brother Esau should have received, because he had exchanged it for a plate of lentils.

As can be deduced from these texts, the blessing at that time was not considered as trivial as it is today, when not even the priest is asked for a blessing in the street.

The blessing for the ancients was even more important than the material inheritance that their parents could leave them, since it was understood that the spiritual blessing included the pecuniary inheritance. Likewise, the Holy Scriptures also declare the gigantic power of the curse, and even affirm that the slavery that humiliated so many races for centuries came from the curse that Noah pronounced on his son Ham, in Genesis 9, 25-ss.

The word of man has a power that he has never calculated and that power he has because we participate in the likeness of God, and if the word of God had power to create all things, God having given man the power to dominate his creation, then the word of man will have power over the creation of God. Hence, when a man blesses or curses, he is opening a door in the life of another man so that, in the case of blessings, all the beneficent power of God can enter into action and, in the case of curses, he will set in motion all the gears of the destructive and torturing power of the evil one in the life of the one who is cursed. That is why the Bible warns us so many times, as in Romans 12:14, that it is not even licit for us Catholics to curse our enemies.

In order to show the satanic power of the curse, I would like to mention the case that came to my knowledge of a man who, after having had a farm with thousands of cultivated hectares full of cattle, ended up practically in misery, only because some of his employees cursed him when he had to throw them out with a simple phrase such as: "I hope to see you and your children begging for bread under a bridge some day". These words, like those of Noah, unleashed the wickedness of men and Satan's malice in such a way that over the years this man lost all his land, crops and livestock.

Note that although we do not believe that our words have so much power, this does not mean that it is so, for I want my readers to consider why in the Old Testament, even the enemies of Israel, paid prophets like Balaan (Numbers 24:10) to curse their enemies, how much was their confidence in the words of a man, especially a man who had powers from God!

Such importance does Holy Scripture give to the power of the curse, that it goes so far as to affirm in Galatians 3:13, that Christ came to rescue us from the curse of the law, making himself accursed for us, and by the mouth of the prophet Malachi 3:9, in which God himself declares, "Ye are accursed from the curse, because ye defraud me, even the whole nation."

In order that we may see graphically the power of the curse to take away a blessing from God, I will relate what happened to one of my servants in Argentina.

This pious woman lived by selling watch batteries in a street stall. She told me that every day she put her earnings in a little box with a holy card of the Sacred Heart of Jesus attached to it, and that the Lord blessed her abundantly, since on several occasions she had noticed that having deposited only one hundred Argentinean pesos, she had paid for services, the market and other necessities for more than $250, but there came a time when her money stopped working and, contrary to what used to happen, she could no longer do with two hundred pesos half of the things she used to do with one hundred.

Surprised that the Lord had stopped blessing her, she prayed asking Him to reveal to her the reason why her economy was being tragically affected. The Lord showed her that the reason for her misfortune was that she had collected fifty pesos owed to her with such lack of charity that the person who had given it to her had returned it to her with hatred, resentment and curse. So in the face of such a fault, Jesus had had to suspend the flow of his economic blessings. Needless to say, this pious woman immediately grabbed that fifty peso bill she still had in her box and took it running to her parish priest as an offering of atonement, and from that moment on the blessed economy she used to enjoy was restored.

With these cited examples I want my readers to reflect on the lack of importance we are currently giving to the power that the curse has, and to change our way of thinking before we are affected by the curse or affect others with our words. That is why I invite you to go deeper into the power that the curse had for the Jewish people, meditating on the book of Numbers 5, 11-31, where it is used as a method to settle an accusation of adultery. Of course, in this modern world, in which adultery has become a sport, this way of judging these crimes may even seem irri-sory, for if we were now to use the method that God gave Moses to discover adulteries, we would certainly run out of the blessed curse water in the face of so many cases to be solved. But we are not discussing here about the effectiveness of the method, but about the importance that the power of the curse has for our God, because it was understood that no woman was going to risk contracting the curses of God through the priest if she was guilty of the crime, because it existed in the conscience that the curse has the power to end the health, with the patrimony and even with the life of a person. This belief was embodied in the sayings "curse of cure has no cure" and "curse of cure certain death".

And it is not that now in our time, our words have ceased to have such force, but it is we who have ceased to be cautious in speaking, and it is sad to see how even within the same people who consider themselves practitioners of the Catholic faith, the words of the apostle James (3:10) are verified, they say that blessing and cursing come from the same mouth, which should not be, at least. This should not be so, at least not among those of us who believe that the Word of God cannot deceive us, and that just because we do not understand the realities contained therein, it does not mean that we should lose respect and reverence for it.

I remember that in the course of my life on several occasions I have heard stories in which women who have pronounced in moments of anger against their children words like: "I wish you would die, you damn brat, because I've had enough of you", have had to cry before the corpse of their children who have suffered tragic death by accident.

And this is because these women are unaware of the power that the curse can give Satan to destroy their own homes. Moreover, they themselves sometimes bring ruin or despair upon their husbands, because they do nothing but fulminate them with curses when they see them spending their wealth on alcohol or vices. This warning that I want to give is for all of us to think twice before opening our mouths against our own and to meditate on texts like Ecclesiasticus 3:9, where it is affirmed: "The blessing of the father strengthens the house of the children, and the curse of the mother destroys the foundations".

But the destructive power of the curse is not limited only to parents and children, but can also affect siblings, and even friends. To give an example of this I cite the case of a young woman, who told me that her brother pronounced the following curse on her, at the moment when she had refused to lend him some money he needed because he had no job: "I hope the same thing happens to you as happened to me and you have to beg for money because you have no job". Days after this simple curse, the young woman was left without work for a period of several months, having to go through many hardships. So much so that until the savings she had and all her liquidation were exhausted, she could not get a job again.

I want to clarify that the closer the bond of consanguinity or sentimental link with the person who is cursed, the greater the force with which Satan will deploy his power to torture the victim of such a curse. Therefore, one should not become paranoid about the fact of having received the curse from a stranger in the street whom one could not help with alms, because certainly the lack of a blood or sentimental link greatly reduces the effectiveness of the words, although I must accept that they are not totally innocuous.

Care and treatment

In the case of having pronounced a curse, we must proceed as St. Francis of Assisi proceeded when he cursed the one who had made war on him within his own congregation, who as penance and reparation spent his time blessing every creature that crossed his path during that day, and therefore it is necessary that we proceed to bless the person that in the moment of anger we cursed, with words more or less like the following:

Prayer to undo a pronounced curse

Lord Jesus, I ask you to forgive me for having pronounced curses with the same mouth with which I commune your Body and Blood, which are the source of every blessing, and I ask that by the same merits of your Body and Blood you bless the soul, body, mind, health, work, economy, family and projects of all those whom I cursed".

In the case of having received a curse, we will proceed as follows: we will try to increase our alms to the poor, and when the poor person answers us: "May God bless him", we will answer: "Lord, may this blessing dissolve every curse that has fallen on me, on my loved ones or on my patrimony, so be it".

The reason why the blessing of the poor is so important to undo the curse of our enemies is because Jesus Christ affirms in the Gospel that what we do to the poor we do to Him, therefore it implies that what the poor do to us also proceeds from Him.

Hence it is my opinion that when a Catholic is approached by a beggar and asks for alms with the words "For the love of God, may I...", in conscience we should not refuse such a request, because the blessing that follows also comes from God.

But in the case that, due to a lack of religious culture, the beggar proceeds to curse the person who denies him the help, that curse could also come from God, according to each circumstance.

I conclude by inviting my readers to think that if blessings are so beneficial and protective and are so easy to obtain, just by giving a generous alms, why risk accumulating curses, either from the poor or from our enemies, which will reach pernicious levels for our life, if we do not cancel them by opposing them with the blessings of the grateful poor.

THE SATANIC POWER OF FEAR

I have seldom heard people talk about the power of fear, even though more than one hundred and fifty texts in Sacred Scripture speak about fear. We must begin by differentiating between two types of fear that are defined in Sacred Scripture. One that is good and highly recommended to practice, and another that is pernicious and must be avoided at all costs.

The fear that is beneficial and should always be carried in the heart is the fear of God. Which is not a fear of God as a destroyer or punisher, but consists in a filial fear, which feels resentful of hurting his paternal heart with sin, therefore it is very different from the panic that the slave feels, of being discovered in contempt to the orders of his master, because he knows that he will be punished with rigor.

Whoever is founded on the fear of God, should never ever fear creatures, because if God is on our side, since we have not offended Him, then who can be against us? That is why the book of Sirach 4:14 says: "He who fears the Lord fears nothing and is not afraid.

152

Thus, in many verses of the Bible we are assured that whoever is founded on the faith of God should not and cannot be afraid, to cite some examples in the Letter to the Hebrews 13, 6, says: "The Lord is my help, I will not fear", and in Psalm 118, 6, "The Lord is with me I will not fear. What can man do to me?", and the Lord insists through the prophet Jeremiah 1, 8, where he says: "Do not be afraid of them, for I am with you to save you".

All these texts and many others that we will not quote here, so as not to be too long, the Lord puts in his word to strengthen the heart of man, because He knows that since ancient times man has nourished a lot of fears that deviated him from the true faith.

Here is where we want to draw the reader's attention to the triple satanic power that fear possesses, namely: first, it hinders and on many occasions disables man's faith; second, it leads to sin; third, fear makes us sick and opens us to the destructive action of Satan and leaves us vulnerable to his evil. Let us briefly explain each of these consequences of fear: first, that it incapacitates faith, as we can see in the case of Peter, who in the fear of the rising tide "became afraid and began to sink", and the Lord rebukes him saying: "O man of little faith, why do you doubt?" Matthew 14:30, with which the scared scripture shows that there is a close link between fear and doubt, because of all that we have said previously, one who is funded in GOD will necessarily be immune to fear.

That is why in Romans 8, 15, it says: "You did not receive the Spirit as slaves to fall back into fear", which means that whoever does not possess the freedom that gives confidence in God ends up being a slave to fear. For faith in God is based on trust, just as doubt is based on fear, therefore it will be a logical deduction that the more trust in God we have, the more faith we will have, and therefore the greater works we will be able to do. Hence such phrases as: "I can do all the things through Christ who strengthens me", Philippians 14:13. "We are more than conquerors through him who loved us",

Romans 8:37, "God gave us not a spirit of Coward but of Power", 2 Timothy 1:7.

Let us now turn to the second power that fear has and that is to of leading to sin. We see this clearly in ancestral religions, where the ancients begin to worship everything that causes them fear; for example: storms, lightning, darkness, earthquakes, volcanoes, many of which were sometimes offered human sacrifices to appease their supposed "divine" wrath. We could affirm that all superstitions have their origin in some fear, for example: not to pass under a ladder, that a black cat does not cross or not to break mirrors. All these types of superstitions that God forbids because they enslave man and separate him from his rationality, are based on a supposed harm or evil that is received when performing such acts, that is why it is so important that we remember here what the book of Proverbs 16, 6 says, "with the fear of God evil is avoided". We could say that all idolatrous religions have their origin in the inordinate fear of the occult, therefore, man ends up constructing imaginary gods to defend him against the things he fears the most, such as plagues, death, diseases, attacks of the spirits of darkness, etc.

On the other hand, we can affirm that fear of God is also a consequence of sin, because as Adam says in Genesis 3, 10: "I was afraid and hid myself", therefore we see that here a bidirectional relationship is established, since fear leads to sin and sin produces fear.

The third of the consequences of fear is that it causes illness, in such a way that the psychology manuals catalog a number of phobias that terribly reduce the freedom of the people who suffer from them. Thus, for example, there are people who are unable to speak in public because of laliophobia or are afraid of being poisoned as toxicophobia, likewise there are people who panic about corpses or death thanks to necrophobia, or there are people who are afraid of being touched because of aphophobia, and all this multitude of fears can degenerate into the worst of all fears, which

154

is pantophobia, which is fear of everything, or otherwise it is a state of pure fear.

With the three previous sections I think that would be enough to show that fear is contrary to God, since we have only seen that they produce bad things in our lives, and we have concluded that fear is a consequence of sin and even a cause, but now we are going to affirm that fear is sin and we base ourselves on the words of John 4:18, "fear carries punishment within it".

In order to see more clearly the power that fear has to allow God to release the destructive malice of Satan because of him, I invite all my readers to analyze the book of Job in its first two chapters, where we are told that Job was a just man, with integrity, upright, fearful of God, separated from evil and that he complied with all the prescriptions of the law. It is therefore uncertain what was the cause for God to allow Satan's devastating action on Job's possessions, on his children and even on his own health. At first one is tempted to think that the cause of such a divine procedure is to give us a lesson about the faithfulness to God of the holy Job, despite the fact that Satan tested him so mercilessly; but if we carefully analyze the text, we find that Job did give a reason to God to suspend his hedge of protection and this was precisely the sin of fear. It is Job himself who confesses it in Job 3:25: "What I fear happens to me and what I am afraid of happens to me", therefore God withdraws his blessings from Job, because although he kept the commandments, he did so for fear that God would abandon him and therefore his fear of God was not authentic, but based on a greater fear of the devil. Hence, in Job we see realized the affirmation of the book of Sirach 27:3, which says: "Whoever does not hold fast to the fear of the Lord will soon see his house destroyed".

If we all analyze the most tragic events of our lives, we will always find that our fear was greater than the trust we had in God at the moment we suffered the misfortune.

Hence, we recommend to all our readers to work ardently to strengthen their trust in God, especially those who plan to dedicate themselves to the ministry of deliverance, because if they leave the slightest crack to Satan, as Job did, he will not hesitate to destroy our patrimony, family and our own health. That is why James, in his letter 4, 7, says: "Submit yourselves to God and face the devil who will flee from you", for the apostle knew that firm trust in God drives back the enemy of souls. That is why hell works tirelessly to foment fear among men.

Therefore, one of the most sublime apostolates that exists is that of preaching confidence in God, as an antidote against sin, sickness, unbelief and the devil himself. If this were done in this way, there would not be so many cowardly priests and bishops who fear the devil and who disguise their fear behind a veneer of rationalism and erudition.

I remember a woman who had a daughter with a clear case of possession, who traveled her country from bishopric to bishopric looking for someone to attend of his daughter. This woman claimed that some bishops had told her that they did not mess with the devil, because suddenly the devil was messing with them. My personal reflection is: "with shepherds like that, no need for wolves".

By way of conclusion of this chapter I bring to mind the change in Job's life when he realized his unfounded fear of the devil and transformed it into a genuine fear of the Lord, who returned to him a hundredfold all that he had allowed the devil to take from him. Therefore, one of the main elements to achieve deliverance in cases where it seems impossible to undo the works of witchcraft, should be more intensified in injecting confidence in God to the person who suffers the evil, rather than concentrating on removing the evil itself, because as long as fear does not disappear, Satan will never disappear from the life of a Child of God.

THE INTERGENERATIONAL FORCE OF SIN

Most Catholics believe that all trials, temptations, and sufferings are caused by our own sins, but we are not always the sole culprits. I remember having to attend to a person who had struggled all their life to earn a living honestly, yet they constantly faced obstacles in their job opportunities and business ventures. This phenomenon caused a great deal of distress for the person because, as we all know, the Lord promises prosperity to those who are faithful in their hearts and follow His laws. This person did not see these promises fulfilled in their life, even though she strived tremendously to keep her tithes, confession and frequent masses, and to stay in the presence of God.

When they consulted me about their situation, they mentioned that they couldn't find any sins in their life that would justify such economic ruin they found themselves in, as they had remained faithful to the path of faith since childhood. I asked them if anyone in their household could have incurred an economic curse by engaging in practices such as witchcraft, spiritualism, or superstitions.

And, above all, I asked her if any other family member was experiencing the same economic hardship as her. She replied that she would answer the first part of the question later, as she needed to investigate, but regarding the financial struggles of her relatives, she could tell me that everyone she knew in her family was in the same miserable situation, despite all their attempts to pursue professional careers and engage in business ventures to improve their circumstances.

In response to this, I assured her that she should look into her ancestors and see if there was someone who had been deeply involved in superstitions or had squandered God's financial blessings in vice. If it affected everyone in general, it would indicate an ancient root.

Indeed, the investigations revealed that a great-grandfather had practiced witchcraft and had consigned all future generations to poverty, as long as Satan kept him wealthy during his lifetime.

Needless to say, it is a challenging task to remove such a deep-seated curse that affects such a large number of people, who, as a result of their ancestor's superstitions and idolatry, they lacked at this moment of faith in God.

Therefore, we began with prayers renouncing witchcraft, doing so in the name of that ancestor. We continued with breaking all the pacts and consecrations that had been made to Satan, and concluded with intergenerational breaking Masses. It should be noted that the effectiveness of this process depended on the number of family members affected by that consecrations, who were willing to pray together as a family to undo the works of the great-grandfather.

It is possible that many of my readers may feel uncertain upon hearing that we affirm the sins of our ancestors can affect us, as it may seem unjust to pay for something we did not do.

For those who may think this way, let us propose the following reflections: First, we must consider that until this day and until the last human being inhabiting this earth, we bear the consequences of the sin of our first parents, Adam and Eve, such as sickness, pain, and death. Additionally, let us cite Exodus 20:5 and 34:7, where it is stated that God is a jealous God, and while it is said that He is slow to anger and rich in mercy, it is also affirmed that He punishes the sins of the fathers on the children, up to the third and fourth generation, when the parents have hated their God and preferred idolatry. Therefore, when worldly pleasures become a substitute for God in a person's life and establish themselves in their hearts as idolatrous worship, as in the case of witches and sorcerers who worship Satan, or the lustful who worship licentiousness, or the ambitious and greedy who worship money, all these sins of idolatry will indeed be punished in the children up to the third and fourth generation. Moreover, depending on the consciousness and malice with which these idols are worshipped, the number of generations affected by God's wrath will be greater.

This affirmation is further supported by Numbers 14:18, which states, "The Lord is slow to anger and abounding in steadfast love, forgiving iniquity and transgression, but he will by no means clear the guilty, visiting the iniquity of the fathers on the children, to the third and the fourth generation."

The reason behind God's actions is that sin is a kind of spiritual illness that is transmitted in a similar way to certain physical diseases such as leukemia, cancer, or circulatory problems. Just as individuals who inherit such physiological anomalies from their parents cannot complain about the injustice of inheriting a disease, we also cannot claim that it is unjust to inherit a spiritual illness due to the misdeeds of our parents. If we view one as a law of the material nature, we must see the other as a law of the spiritual nature. Furthermore, as we mentioned before, the fact that physical diseases can be inherited is a direct consequence of the original sin of Adam and Eve, who lost their impassivity by transgressing God's law.

The only thing God wants to achieve with this approach is to make us aware that our sins have consequences not only on a personal level but also on a familial, social, and even universal scale. However, even with this knowledge, God cannot make mankind reconsider and refrain from sinning.

This spiritual discovery has generated numerous books and reflections within the Catholic Renewal movement regarding the intergenerational power of sin. If we analyze human history, we will find that this punishment from God manifests as being born with a tendency to sin in the same manner as our parents did. For example, in our families or in families we know, we may find that the children or grandchildren of someone who took their love for intoxicating drinks to the extreme end up becoming alcoholics, prioritizing these substances over their own life and health.

Similarly, the children of bisexual parents are born with a tendency towards homosexuality, and the same goes for the children of thieves, deviants, and the greedy, among others. It doesn't mean that one is obliged to sin in the same manner as their parents did, but the strength and attraction towards these sins will be greater than in the general population.

One of the consequences of intergenerational sins is that they give more power to curses and evil desires when they occur among relatives. As mentioned in a previous chapter, we cited the case of a fifteen-year-old girl who we had to attend to because she was possessed by demons. Although the girl herself had not committed any sins related to superstition or evoking the dead – in fact, she was an innocent victim who acquired the spiritual possession – it was all due to her grandmother, who was the one performing the evil acts directed towards her daughter-in-law, the girl's mother. The mother, thanks to her spiritual strength and her practice of the Catholic faith, was immune to her mother-in- law's curse. However, God allowed the evil to pass intergenerationally to the granddaughter, who was greatly cherished by the witch grandmother, in an attempt to make the wicked grandmother reconsider her actions by witnessing the suffering of this innocent child. Unfortunately, those who work for Satan are so obstinate that they are not even moved by such displays of pain.

From this example, we can conclude that acts of wickedness that occur among family members will unleash Satan's wrath with even greater violence and they allow him to act more freely because God understands that greater wickedness is required to desire harm to one's own flesh and blood than to wish it upon a stranger.

Another consequence of this type of sin is that undoing its effects is more challenging. It requires the unity of faith among the majority or all of those affected to counteract the evil caused by an ancestor.

Care and Treatment

That's why I conclude this reflection on the intergenerational force of sin by using my own family as an example of how to break the chains of our ancestors' sins. It seems that one of our ancestors, perhaps due to embezzlement, greed, or squandering of money, had created an economic binding in my siblings and me, hindering the dignified pursuit of our respective professions and fair compensation. For instance, one of my brothers is an electrical engineer and could barely make a living selling cold cuts in a business he had started to sustain himself. My older brother, on the other hand, is a graphic designer and managed to get by with occasional advertising work from home, but neither of them had landed any significant projects in ten years. As for my third brother, although he had a job, he couldn't sell an apartment to pay off the house he had purchased. We decided to gather as a family every Sunday, with their wives and children, to pray the Rosary solely and exclusively for the breaking of intergenerational chains, pleading to the Virgin Mary for her intercession.

The agreement was that members who couldn't be present would offer the Rosary from wherever they were for the same intention, and when I was present, we would celebrate the Holy Mass for the breaking of those chains.

After four months of consistently engaging in this intergenerational prayer group, we clearly witnessed positive consequences. My brother, the electrical engineer, landed a job with an oil company. The graphic designer started working as a commercial manager for a security company, and the other brother was able to sell his apartment to pay off the house he had bought. The fact that there were three positive outcomes from these family prayers demonstrates that it was not a mere coincidence but rather the untying of something that mysteriously bound the disloyalties of our ancestors to God's law.

For those considering initiating this type of family prayer for the breaking of intergenerational sins, it's important to note that the success of such prayer depends first and foremost on the faith and conviction of each family member participating in this spiritual endeavor. It can greatly hinder progress if one family member attends reluctantly or under obligation, or even if they disdain the invitation to pray due to disbelief.

Secondly, the effectiveness also depends on concentrating the prayers on the sin that has affected the greatest number of family members, because many times we start praying for the economy, because some want to improve their situation and we do not take into account that perhaps the number of unbelievers or superstitious people is greater and that we should first pray that they enter the path of faith and renounce Satan, or in other words, that we first worry about the spiritual riches of our families before worrying about the material ones.

Finally, one of the main elements of such prayers should be perseverance in it, no matter that at first no palpable change is seen in the family situation or that the changes that are given apparently undo themselves, because many times the forces of darkness will try to impede the devotion and gratitude of the family by undoing or snatching away the goods achieved. But if one perseveres in spite of these attacks, there will come a time when God will grant fruits that will persevere in spite of the intentions of the prince of this world.

Prayer for Breaking Intergenerational Chains

In the mighty name of Jesus Christ, the Lord, by the grace of God, with the power of the blood of the Lamb of God, His glorious wounds, and His Holy Cross. With the absolute and total power of the Holy Trinity; with the strength and power of the Holy Spirit, with the power of the Blessed Virgin Mary, with the power of the patriarch Saint Joseph, and with the power of the Holy Archangels Saint Michael, Saint Gabriel, and Saint Raphael, our Holy Guardian Angel and the Celestial Court.

I break and dissolve every curse, enchantment, seal, spell, witchcraft, bond, trap, snare, trickery, lie, stumbling block, obstacle, deception, deviation or distraction, spiritual influence or chain, desire for ruin; also every illness of our body, soul, and mind, that has been conjured upon me, upon my loved ones, upon my belongings, or upon anything that may harm me, for the sins or mistakes of my past generations, for the envy of my enemies, or for my own sins or mistakes.

In the name of Jesus Christ, the Lord, by the power of His glorious wounds and His Holy Cross, I break and dissolve every chain of sins of pride, lust, envy, greed, gluttony, sloth, or wrath committed by my parents, my grandparents, my great-grandparents, my great- great-grandparents, and all the other generations, up to the first one recorded in the book of life, that may be affecting me in my actions or in my spiritual or social life. I ask our Lord Jesus to set a barrier of His precious Body and Blood that prevents the offenses, guilt, and punishments that my ancestors may have deserved from affecting me or my future descendants.

Now I place the Cross of Jesus Christ between myself and all the generations of my family tree, and I claim in the name of Jesus Christ that there be no direct communication between any of these generations and myself, nor with my loved ones or my belongings.

All communication will be filtered through the Precious Blood of Jesus, which we claim descend upon us, to permeate us, to surround us, and to isolate us in such a way that it

163

drives away from us every unclean spirit that seeks to disturb us or any force or influence originating from them.

May there only be room within us for the light, truth, love, and peace of our Lord Jesus Christ. Immaculate Mary, clothe me with the light, power, anointing, and strength of your faith. Eternal Father, please command the Holy Archangels, Angels, and all the Saints to assist us from now on. Thank you, Jesus, for your Blood and for your life, and for being my wisdom, my righteousness, my sanctification, and my redemption. I surrender to the mystery of your Holy Spirit and receive with respect and reverence your true sealing, covering, and protection.

Oh, Archangel Saint Michael, illuminate us with your light, protect us with your wings, and defend us with your sword and shield. Amen.

THE RECIDIVISM

At this point in my book, readers must have formed a clear idea of the modus operandi of witchcraft and how a person can achieve liberation through the prayers of the Church. Although in the next chapter we will conclude with some recommendations, as a method, on how to proceed to attain freedom, before that, we must discuss a phenomenon that must be taken into account when seeking liberation from all diabolical oppression, and that is the issue of recidivism from two perspectives: first, the recidivism of enemy attacks, and second, the recidivism in sin on the part of the person who has been liberated.

Speaking of the first type of recidivism, I must say that in all the years I have been fighting against witchcraft, I have observed that it is a constant fact that when a person is going through the process of breaking free from all the evils that afflict them, the witches or sorcerers somehow spiritually become aware that their malefic work has been broken, either alerted by the person who did the work and found out that the victim has been freed from satanic influence or by the very infernal spirit that alerts them because the liberated person has slipped out of their clutches. From this announcement, the agent of iniquity will renew witchcraft and, if possible, will cast an even stronger spell with the aim of discouraging the person so that they suspend their liberation or to mislead the priest or layperson who is performing the prayers, making them think that they are useless in that case. Therefore, both the one performing the liberation and the one undergoing the process to attain their freedom must take this fact into account, so as not to be distracted or discouraged, for as the Lord says, the one who perseveres until the end will be saved. The key point here is to maintain the firm belief that Jesus Christ is the victor and that the defeat of Satan and his empire has been prophesied for a thousand years. Therefore, in the ministry of liberation, one must have great creativity and live in a continuous creation of spiritual strategies, without clinging to any specific one, for in spiritual warfare we will find that prayers that were very effective in some cases are useless in others. In other cases, we will witness the breaking of chains simply by redirecting the victim to make a good confession and by frequent use of the sacraments, while there will be people who have attended hundreds of liberation masses without notable progress in their process. Hence, ingenuity and being guided by the Holy Spirit through His charisms are a fundamental part of the effectiveness of our procedures.

Regarding this point, I just want to add that as long as there is a change in the person's condition, and when I say change, I don't necessarily mean improvement; that is, even if the person's situation worsens, this indicates to us that the prayers we are making are having an effect, and therefore we should not immediately change or abandon them, as the worsening is a symptom that we have already broken something that the infernal forces are not only renewing but trying to intensify. Therefore, it would be a mistake to suspend a method just because it appears that we are regressing when, in reality, we are encountering new evils because we have already imperceptibly achieved several victories.

We should only vary the prayers or the method we are using if we see that the liberation sessions pass without any substantial change, for better or worse. If the change is for the worse, we must consider the affected person and avoid subjecting them to excessively draining sessions to prevent creating weariness. There are moments when the reactions are so violent that the person experiencing them feels it is a kind of spiritual martyrdom. Even though they may want to multiply these sessions out of anxiety and desperation to rid themselves of these evils, the person leading the process must prevent the emotional exhaustion of the victim by encouraging them to take breaks and offering their inner sufferings as expiation for their own sins, those of their ancestors, and those of the enemies who have caused them harm.

There is another type of recidivism that, to me, is the most concerning, and I will illustrate it with a case that happened to me in Argentina. It involves a woman who, out of desperation to not lose her husband, had undergone some Umbanda rituals, which led to her becoming diabolically possessed. She was in a state of despair because a legion of demons resided within her.

I took the case and with great enthusiasm, we embarked on the task of evicting that troop from the infernal army that was tormenting the poor woman. The struggle was arduous, and the fatigue and exhaustion, both of the servants of the Lord and the possessed, as well as my own, I would dare say, were exaggerated. The sessions were worthy of a military epic, where numerous principalities and powers manifested themselves, refusing to retreat because the woman had given them permission to enter by seeking a solution to her emotional conflicts through witchcraft. After months of relentless battle, the Lord showed us that the woman had been set free. We sang victory, congratulated ourselves, exchanged felicitations, and each went about their personal duties. But these joys were not going to last long, for a few weeks later, the woman called me again, saying that she felt the same or even worse. Obviously, I reassured her, explaining that it was normal for witches to renew their witchcraft in an attempt to discourage us, but I asked her to come to my office, where I would say a prayer to try to break what had been renewed, as typically, once the main elements have been broken, the renewals of spells, although they may have more intense manifestations, are often much easier to break, especially if everything is done while remaining in a state of grace, as the newly invoked evils have nowhere to take root.

However, in this case, my astonishment reached its peak when, as I began the prayer, the demons manifested themselves again, and when I asked them to identify themselves, they said that they were no longer a legion but now two. Immediately, I suspended the liberation prayers and called her by name, bringing her out of the trance, and I recited the words of the Lord from Luke 11:24-26.

"When an unclean spirit comes out of a man, it passes through arid places seeking rest and does not find it. Then it says, 'I will return to the house I left.' On its arrival, it finds the house swept clean and put in order. Then it goes and brings seven other spirits more evil than itself, and they enter and dwell there. And the final condition of that man is worse than the first."

I conveyed to the woman that, analyzing this text and seeing that she now had two legions instead of one, my verdict was that she must have relapsed into some sin. This multiplication of unclean spirits was only possible because the first ones expelled had found the house swept clean and put in order due to the transgression of God's law, allowing them to enter accompanied by spirits worse than the first. She vehemently denied it and even took offense at my assertion. However, seeing that I remained firm in my position, she had to admit that she had indeed committed a fault and ended up saying to me, "I went to get my fortune read to find out if I had been completely liberated."

Needless to say, upon hearing such a statement, and making an effort to contain my anger at such foolishness, I simply said, "Go to that witch who read your fortune and ask her to cast out the demons. For I was not willing to continue wasting my time on someone who did not have a sufficiently mature and sane judgment to abide by the instructions I had given." So, no plea or tears could move me to pray for her again, up to this day.

That is why I often tell many mothers who insist that I pray for deliverance for their children against their will, that if I cast out the demons and they continue in their sin of unbelief, instead of doing them good, I will do them harm. Because those spiritual entities will return with even worse ones, and instead of seeing positive changes in their children, they will witness them becoming more and more influenced by Satan every day. Therefore, in these cases, it is advisable to simply entrust them to God and celebrate a holy Mass for them, hoping that God's mercy will pour into their hearts, opening their eyes to the evil that possesses them.

Chapter X

Conclusions

Before concluding, I cannot stress enough to all my readers that turning to any form of these magics has catastrophic spiritual consequences that a Catholic will eventually discover. What I say is because when a person turns to Satan to obtain some benefit, they prostitute themselves in the eyes of God, as Deuteronomy 20:6 states. It opens the doors to the agent of evil to harm them in the future, whether in their own health, their economy, or even their own children up to the third and fourth generation. My experience tells me that it is not enough to confess such a sin, as confession obtains forgiveness from God. However, despite this, I have found that the devil still possesses a certain power to affect and harm the one who committed such a sin, and he will use that power when the person attempts to truly convert and walk the path of salvation.

Hence, many people claim that while they were on the path of perdition, the devil never bothered them. But the moment they attempted to convert and walk in holiness, the devil hindered their finances, destroyed their marriage that had no inconveniences while they were in concubinage, or led astray children who were moderately good until they began to walk in the ways of the Lord. These issues were not resolved until they sincerely renounced Satan and witchcraft, demanding that the devil, in the name of Jesus Christ, return any pact, consecration, power, or authority he had over them due to the sins of superstition and idolatry committed when seeking witches and fortune-tellers.

Therefore, as a summary in these conclusions, we present the steps to be taken once this entire book has been read and there is a well-founded belief that one is under the influence of a hex or spell:

- Pray as we said in the previous chapter to break the intergenerational chains and thus make sure that the sins of our ancestors are not giving Satan a greater force of action than that which is given to him by the ma-lefice that we think is affecting us.

- Once our intergenerational antecedents have been cleansed, we will proceed to renounce witchcraft, which we placed in chapter III, in the case that we have gone to the witches, even though many years have passed since we committed and confessed that sin, in order to remove the power that we gave it with our own faults.

- To break all the curses that we have pronounced and that have been able to be returned against us, or all those that have been pronounced against us as it was said in chapter IX.

- The frequency of sacraments should be increased, especially confession and the Eucharist, since the Eucharist is like a bulletproof vest against witchcraft. Hence, it is enough for a normal Catholic to go to Mass on Sundays, just as it is enough for a normal policeman to put on his vest during a special operation. But the Catholic who is sure that he has been wronged must receive communion daily, just as a soldier who is at war must wear his vest every day as a matter of life and death.

- The prayer of the holy rosary is primordial in a process of liberation, but the intention for which one prays should be restricted only and exclusively to the intention of attaining liberation, because when many intentions are placed, the intensity of the act of faith is divided in all the proposed

170

intentions, and as we said, to break witchcraft, the important thing is the intensity of the act of faith.

- Use the sacramentals water, salt and exorcised oil, not in a superstitious and talismanic way, but in the manner described in chapter II. Analyze with balance and equanimity the reactions that one has when applying them.

- Do until you reach some improvement the prayers that we recommend according to the type of evil spell of which you think you are affected, because sometimes, although the person thinks to be affected by a type of magic, sometimes its origin may be in another and that is why you should not go to the next point, until you have identified what type of evil spell you are under, according to the reactions you have to the prayers you make.

- If full recovery is not achieved through the above points, an exorcist priest may be called in, specifying how they have tried to address their problem and how far they have been able to advance in improvement without being able to achieve full recovery.

- In case you are unable to get an exorcist priest, seek out a Catholic Charismatic Renewal prayer group and ask there people who have charisms of the Holy Spirit to give you new guidance on how to continue to handle the situation, according to what the Lord shows you in prayer.

- Do not limit yourself to only one opinion and be very careful that they are truly people of God and not the famous "very nice ladies, who in reality are witches who barricade themselves behind an image of the Virgin or the Angels".

- Finally, if you have not already exhausted all hopes, try to contact us through our website:
  www. victoriadelacruz.com.

Epilogue

The bishops of the Catholic Church, for the most part, have allowed themselves to be infected by rationalism to such an extent that they no longer even fear denying the existence of the devil or asserting, at best, that the ministry of exorcism is unnecessary. According to them, all the diabolical manifestations claimed by people can be resolved through psychiatric treatment.

For them and for all those who doubt the existence of the devil, it should be assured that the reality of diabolical possessions being healed through prayers, even when done remotely, cannot be denied. This can be seen in the case of Saint Gema Galgani, whose spiritual director performed exorcisms on her while he was in Rome and she was in Lucca.

If it were a psychological illness, it would require at least the presence of the patient so that the necessary suggestion could be created as a therapy to produce the normalization or psychic stability of the person.

Most people think that no one can perform an exorcism without being authorized by the bishop of a diocese, but in reality, Jesus says in Luke 9:49-50 and Mark 9:38-40 that it should not be prevented. We must understand the restrictions of the Church hierarchy in this way, that whoever wants to exercise the ministry in the name of the Catholic Church and using the official rituals that the Church has, must have the approval of a bishop to prevent excesses and damages that may be caused. But at no time can the Church restrict the liberation prayer exercised by Protestant pastors, by Catholic priests and faithful, if the prayer being made is not part of the ritual, nor is it done in the name of the Church, but by virtue of the charisms received from Christ and the authorization given by

Jesus when he says, "Go into all the world and cast out demons." For if they were to prohibit it, they would not be acting as representatives of Christ, but as antagonists of Christ who commands the expulsion of demons as one of the clearest signs that the kingdom of God is among us and that defeating the devil was one of the main reasons that moved the Son of God to become incarnate, since according to 1 John 3:8, the Son of God was revealed to destroy the works of the devil.

It is sad that the pastors of the Catholic Church do not consider the terrible pastoral consequences for the people of God who have been entrusted to them, if a person who feels affected by oppression, obsession, or diabolical possession, upon seeking their bishop's help, is automatically labeled as crazy by said pastor, they will obviously seek a solution to their spiritual problem elsewhere. Let us consider some Bible verses to support what we have said:

God says through the prophet Malachi 3:5, "Then I will draw near to you for judgment. I will be a swift witness against the sorcerers." And in Exodus 22:17, it is commanded to Moses, "You shall not let a sorceress live."

In Deuteronomy 18:10-12, it is stated, "There shall not be found among you anyone who... practices divination, or is a soothsayer, or an augur, or a sorcerer, or one who casts spells, or a medium, or a spiritist, or one who calls up the dead. For whoever does these things is an abomination to the LORD your God."

In Revelation 21:8, it says, "But as for the cowardly... and sorcerers... their place will be in the lake that burns with fire and sulfur, which is the second death."

Revelation 22:15 affirms, "Outside are the dogs and sorcerers... and everyone who loves and practices falsehood." And in Leviticus 20:27, it decrees, "A man or a woman who is a medium or a necromancer shall surely be put to death. They shall be stoned with stones; their blood shall be upon them."

As we can see, these are severe judgments and condemnations for God to impose on something harmless, as it seems that death by stoning or exclusion from the kingdom of heaven are not proportional punishments for something that the majority considers innocuous. Although what I have said is sufficient to refute the claims made by rationalist theologians, regarding the effectiveness of witchcraft, I will continue to argue to fully convince my readers that witchcraft is not a matter we can overlook or ignore without serious consequences for our faith.

In the Holy Scripture, it is clear that sorcerers can possess great powers granted by the forces of the underworld, so much so that they dare to confront the prophets of God. This can be seen in the case of Moses in Egypt when Pharaoh's sorcerers confronted Moses by performing wonders that emulated the miracles God had commanded Moses and Aaron to perform in order to liberate their people.

In Exodus 7:11, it is stated, "Then Pharaoh summoned the wise men and the sorcerers, and they, the magicians of Egypt, also did the same by their secret arts." Those who claim that witchcraft has no efficacy should take note of this affirmation, as they are directly contradicting God's revelation that asserts the Egyptian sorcerers had the power to perform signs similar to those of Moses. Certainly, they could not do everything Moses did, but the wonders they performed are not insignificant.

The Holy Scripture affirms that the sorcerers had the power to transform their staffs into living creatures, such as serpents. Exodus 7:12 states, "Each one threw down his staff and it became a serpent. But Aaron's staff swallowed up their staffs." Likewise, it is stated in Exodus 7:22 that they had the power to turn water into blood through their enchantments. And later, in Exodus 8:7, it is declared that the sorcerers also had the power to summon frogs upon the land of Egypt.

As we have demonstrated with these texts, the rationalistic and irreverent stance currently held by some, which under- mines the faith that has been upheld for centuries, not only within the Catholic Church but even more anciently within the Jewish people, is becoming increasingly unsustainable.

To the shame of these skeptical believers, I remind them that the Catholic Church has included prayers against plagues in its rituals for centuries, invoked by sorcerers. This implies that the faith of the Church has always regarded the power of witches to cause harm as a reality. I myself have witnessed infestations of insects in houses where the possibility of any infestation source, such as garbage, decomposing food, or sewers, has been eliminated. Flies appear in alarming numbers that do not extend to the surrounding areas but only manifest within that specific property. These flies are even immune to conventional insecticides but perish upon contact with exorcised water, which is scientifically inexplicable, as water is not a harmful element to any flying insect.

What I have realized is that Satan's cunning goes beyond what our human intelligence can expect, as these supernatural phenomena tend not to occur in the presence of unbelievers, as Satan is primarily interested in maintaining them in that state. Thus, the children of God, who have power in this world to undo his works, become harmless beings.

I am particularly burdened by the sorrow of the death of a gentleman who was brought to me in an advanced state of illness caused by witchcraft, which was administered to him through food.

I know that what I am about to say may not be believed by many, but I speak for those who have faith. This man had an unexplained abdominal swelling according to the doctors, as they found no medical reason for his deteriorating health. However, when we prayed for him, the poor man would only vomit things he hadn't even eaten on the day we were praying for his deliverance. And through the skin of his abdomen, the head of a pig could be clearly seen moving inside him. As the situation worsened, we decided to act in faith and from a distance, limiting ourselves to blessing the medications prescribed by the doctors and praying over his photo, pleading to God for improvement. Unfortunately, he died weeks later because, from an ecclesiastical standpoint, we were not allowed to intervene with full force in the deliverance of the sick person to avoid legal complications. This is similar to the case of Anneliese Michel, which sparked controversy due to the death of the possessed girl, leading to a trial where the priest was accused of homicide for her death during the exorcism. The incident was even portrayed in a film called "The Exorcism of Emily Rose."

It is sad to see that we are unable to do everything we should due to fears of misunderstanding from both civil and ecclesiastical authorities, and that we have to witness the death of our faithful and hear the sarcastic laughter of the spiritual criminals who are the witches, conjuring death and destruction with their witchcraft practices.

Now that we have finished presenting the evidence of the effectiveness of witchcraft, we should clarify some other notions, especially what we understand by witch or sorcerer and how they differ from other characters found in the occult field, as well as whether they are all inherently evil.

Before we proceed, I want to make a clarification regarding my previous assertion that condemned souls or tormented souls can possess a human being. I recall an exorcist bishop assuring me that, theologically, he couldn't explain this phenomenon since, according to faith, once a human being dies, they go to heaven, purgatory, or hell. However, he encountered this strange phenomenon multiple times during exorcisms and couldn't find any theological basis for it. My response was that I had found a theological basis in the scriptures for this phenomenon. If Jesus said in the Gospel of Luke 20:36 that the children of God who are saved will be like angels in the Kingdom of Heaven, then analogously, we must accept that those who have dedicated themselves to evil will be like demons and therefore possess the same abilities as them in hell.

What I just said serves as a warning to exorcist priests who, in some cases, feel defeated when they see that the ritual has no effect on the demon possessing the person they are attending to. To avoid wasting time, they should change the wording of the ritual to "condemned soul" or "tormented soul," and they will see how the effectiveness of the ritual changes. I have also been deceived several times by these types of souls claiming to be a certain demon when, in reality, they are simply the soul of a deceased sorcerer who has been conjured to do evil from beyond the grave. Due to their degree of wickedness, they have attained the same privileges as a demon.

To illustrate this, I will recount a case that happened to me in the city of Medellin, where a young woman had been taken to every exorcist they knew. None of them had been able to cast out the demon she claimed to be Satan. After long sessions in which they couldn't remove the demon, all the exorcists had given up.

When she was brought to me, I don't like to rely solely on the opinions of the affected individuals, nor do I believe much of what the demons themselves say, as they are princes of lies so I consulted with one of my servant of the Lord who has the gift of spiritual vision, through which God allows him to see the spiritual realities afflicting people. Immediately, he told me that he didn't see Satan in her, but a condemned soul that was bound to the young woman through a blood pact from wrist to wrist.

When I asked the girl if she had made a blood pact with someone who had died, she was greatly surprised that we asked her that question. After some hesitation, during which I told her that if she didn't tell me the truth, I wouldn't help her, she decided to confess that her husband had been a hitman, and they had made a pact that wherever he went, she would go, and wherever she went, he would go. They sealed the pact by cutting their wrists and joining their blood. Soon after, her husband was shot and killed in one of his jobs, without having time to repent.

This explained why my servant of the Lord saw a condemned soul bound to the girl's wrist through a blood pact, the soul of her husband was the one demanding that his wife accompany him to the hell he deserved, and he would not leave until that was accomplished. This also explained the manifestations of screams and desperation that the girl displayed in prayerful and worshipful environments, even during Holy Mass, where she would lose consciousness and reveal what she had inside. That's why the soul of her husband claimed to be Satan, so that the exorcist priests couldn't remove him through the ritual.

I proposed to the girl that the only way to free herself from this oppression was to break the blood pact with her husband's soul at the moment of receiving Holy Communion, by virtue of the Blood of Christ received in the sacrament. The girl refused to do so because she didn't want her husband to go to hell. She revealed that she knew it was him because she could feel his presence at night, even when they were intimate. I explained to her that her refusal to break the pact wouldn't prevent her husband from going to hell, but it would lead her own soul to eternal damnation for having had the opportunity to break the pact and choosing not to do so.

Faced with this clarification, she said she would try to do it, but the level of manifestation from this condemned soul due to the pact was so intense that it made her spit out the Eucharist during the moment of communion. This continued for several days until she managed to reach a level of consciousness where she could forcefully break the blood pact by the power of the Blood of Christ, and thus she was liberated from the possession.

Prayer Index